P9-ECS-654

to David and Trevina
for shared stories,

autrefois –

Laure

May 5 - 2021)

really?

Laure Reichek

Stories

Autrefois
to Today

Published by Creators Equity Foundation
Berkeley, California, USA

This book originally appeared on the internet at
www.reichek.org/Laure (upper-case "L")
Images can be viewed full-size on the internet
by clicking on the images.

Cover photo: Laure at Toby's Barn,
Point Reyes Station, CA, 2019
Photo was taken by an anonymous tourist
and given to Chris Giacomini of Toby's Barn,
who then gave it to Laure.

Director of Publication   Joshua Reichek
Publication Editor   Elizabeth Baker
Primary Editor   Barbara Crum
Self-publishing Printer   UBuildABook

Second Edition
First Printing September 2020
Second Printing March 2021
ISBN 978-0-578-70298-8

Copyright 2020, 2021
Creators Equity Foundation
Berkeley, California, USA

Contents

Laure

Not long ago, not so far away, on the same planet, a man was judged by the quality of his works; a woman, by the way she ran her household. No one was unemployed. There was more work to do than there were hands to do it.

In the town, there was electricity but no running water. Most people had a garden behind their houses and, also, a small vineyard or piece of a forest. Wood and coal were the only sources of energy. In the village, people were craftsmen or shopkeepers.

In the surroundings, the people were farmers with a few cows and pigs, hay and wheat fields. Some families were only tenant farmers or sharecroppers. There was no electricity, running water or sewer systems on the farms. They had a well, candles or kerosene lamps, and went to bed at night knowing what they had to do the next day to sell their surpluses at the Friday market. Women made butter and cheese, clothes. They wore women's clogs around the farms and store-bought shoes on Sundays to go to church, for weddings, dances and funerals.

Laure Reichek née Guyot

There were many festivals with decorated chariots, parades, and dances. Those who lived in the village could go see a movie once a week in the back of the largest café, where men also went to play cards and drink the local rosé wine after the weekly market. There were also cafés in the kitchen of many houses, such as the local barber and bakers.

Each craftsman belonged to a guild—the masons, the carpenters, the winemakers, those who worked metal (the farriers, the clockmakers) had a guild responsible for a festival. The town had a municipal band of volunteers, who would play at each festival and give a concert in the town hall once a year.

There were two times—BEFORE THE WAR TIMES and AFTER THE WAR TIMES—and they were spoken of as such. BEFORE THE WAR meant the way our forefathers had done. AFTER THE WAR meant the American way, i.e., the mechanization of agriculture, thanks to the Marshall Plan—tractors instead of horses and oxen, harvesting machines instead of your neighbors with scythes and sickles, flattening the landscape for large machinery instead of planting hedgerows, barbed wire instead of honeysuckle and blackberry hedges. Mechanization changed everything and took command—cars, trucks, vans, everywhere—super-markets competing with farmers' markets.

Laure Reichek née Guyot

Chateaumeillant, Cher, Berry, France, circa 1950

The rapid expansion of this non-indigenous transformation created an immediate division between those who could afford it and those who could not. Small farms disappeared, old trees were uprooted to flatten the land for the easy movement of machines, country roads were paved. The landscape itself was transformed; landmarks, iconic sites, spiritual and historical anchors disappeared.

What happened DURING the war is under the regime of BEFORE. The landscape has not changed. People have taken sides. Some support the Vichy government—the merchants, the pious, rich farmers. The majority—the

Laure Reichek née Guyot

workers, the poor farmers—support and are in the Resistance (covertly, few overtly before 1943).

This small town had been a Roman stronghold known as MEDIOLANUM—MIDDLE OF THE LAND. Now, how did the Romans know that? No wonder we—the ones they called the HAIRY ONES—were impressed by everything they did. How could one (200 years BC) measure a country? The Romans did—and accurately. The present-day marker indicating the geographic center of France is not very far away from Mediolanum—known today as Chateaumeillant.

It is said that it was a Roman officer from Mediolanum, France, who founded MEDIOLANUM—MILANO—in what is now Italy, after his return to his homeland.

The town has a small museum housing the artifacts found on the site and the surrounding areas by farmers plowing or digging wells and foundations. There is even the burial site (a tumulus) of a high-ranking officer. It is not a pretty town—houses of grey stucco are stuck one next to the other along one main street going north-south with a zigzag in the middle. On a rainy day it looks dismal, sad, even ugly (like most French towns of the 18th century). But if the visitor knows how to get lost in the countryside, he will find the medieval—even Roman—vestiges of its past, the charm of a shy and delicate Nature, the landscapes of George Sand and the "Grand Meaulnes", the swamps of AVARICUM, the

Laure Reichek née Guyot

Cistercian Abbey, the habitat of the many legends, its history.

The town is on a hill, which allowed the Romans to overlook the countryside around their camp. Tunnels dug below their camp led to all sides of the surrounding areas and were large enough to move men, animals and equipment. The remnants of these tunnels still serve today as cellars for the town inhabitants.

As in most villages and small towns in rural France before World War II, there was no running water, no sewer systems. There was electricity in the towns and villages but not in the hamlets. Farms were situated near wells. so water could be drawn, one bucket at a time. No plumbing systems, no bathrooms, no faucets anywhere, wash tubs but no sinks.

There were outhouses, always a distance from the farm, usually past the woodpile so the users of the outhouse could bring back firewood for the fireplace, where cooking was done. Usually, there was a brick and stone oven in one wall, fired once a week to make bread and bake pies and other delicacies. Very few farms had wooden stoves to cook with or heat the room.

Most farms had only one room with a bed arranged against the wall, and a long table with long benches on each side, and a fireplace. The beds, high off the stone floor, were enclosed in tents of heavy flannel attached to the ceiling with a large brass ring. Those curtains

Laure Reichek née *Guyot*

kept in the heat from the bodies and gave a measure of privacy to the occupants. The cloth was often red.

A family consisted of one or two grandparents, their son or daughter, the grandchildren, and the farmhands, often a couple and their children. The land was inherited or was leased to sharecroppers —poor peasants who shared half the products of the farm with absentee owners.

Women knew how to knit and sew clothes. Only men's work clothes were bought, and they lasted a lifetime. Linens were a part of a woman's dowry and lasted more than a generation; they were often of hand-spun, hand-woven cotton or linen. They were washed by boiling in large tubs hung from a tripod placed over a fire outside in the courtyard, then taken in a wheelbarrow to the nearest stream for beating with a paddle, then rinsed in clear running water. Diapers and women's sanitary napkins were treated the same way. Once rinsed and wrung, the laundry was spread on the hedgerows of honeysuckle or blackberry to dry.

There were two schools, one for boys and one for girls; all children had to attend school until the age of fourteen. Farm children had to walk miles each day to come to town on foot. Some stayed with relatives or other families in town during school days. All children had an hour and a half for lunch, since they often had to go fetch water at the three pumps in town during

Laure Reichek née Guyot

their lunch break. The water was carried in tall metal containers with one handle on the side, called *brocs,* that carried about two gallons.

Only a few families in town had radios or wind-up gramophones. There were only 5 telephones in the village: the post office was number 1; the gendarmerie was number 2; the two doctors, Dr. Guyot and Dr. Touraton, were numbers 3 and 4, respectively; and the veterinarian, Mr. Lebrun, was number 5. Each hamlet had a telephone in the café or small post office, from which you could call another post office and tell the operator at what time you would be there to place a call to another person. A boy on a bicycle would relay the message to an isolated farm, and the correspondent would ride on horse or bicycle to the post office or telephone to be there at the appointed time.

When sick or in need of a doctor, patients would just appear at the doctor's door or be brought in. Persons with chronic illnesses would wait for Fridays to visit the doctor after the weekly market and before going to the cafés.

There was one church and one cemetery. Bells would toll loudly enough to inform everyone of funerals or weddings. Those who could afford it paid women to go door-to-door to announce funerals or to serve as "weepers"—women who moaned loudly behind the coffin.

Laure Reichek née Guyot

Communications from the town hall to the people about elections and meetings were made via a drummer who went from neighborhood to neighborhood, hamlet to hamlet, beating a roll from his drum to attract attention and then reading the notices in a loud voice. Since he had a large area to cover on an old bicycle, it would often take several days to deliver messages. He was rewarded with generous quantities of wine to clear his throat after each reading and was obliged to sleep in ditches or barns at the end of the day. Bigoudi was our town drummer and the best-known alcoholic—of which there were many, since wine was easier to get from a bottle than water from a pump or well. But he was part of our landscape and accepted as such.

Laure Reichek née *Guyot*

Larousse
Chateaumeillant, Cher, France, 1937–1945

When I asked Suzanne the difference between a village and a hamlet, she told me that the hamlet was smaller than a village and did not have a church. That answer disturbed me because Jean Sablon, popular crooner of the 20s, had been singing: "Il est une église, au fond d'un hameau, dont le fin clocher se mire dans l'eau, dans l'eau pure d'une riviere." So, a hamlet, according to the song, could have a church. Could it or couldn't it? It bothered me. Papa, who was really my grandfather but had brought me up with Grandma and Suzanne since I was eleven days old, was God. He therefore knew everything worth knowing.

I asked him the difference between a village and a hamlet. He immediately pulled out Volume I of the 1929 Larousse Universel (the latest) and spelling the word loudly several times read the tome's entry: "German origin, related to the English 'home', a group of a few rural houses not incorporated into a larger town." So, there you were—church or no church; Larousse did not say. But Suzanne could not say "no church."

Grandpa took the opportunity to make me repeat the spelling over and over again—H A M E A U. The rhythm suggested a tune that formed in my head and I went back to Suzanne in the kitchen singing H A M E A U

Laure Reichek née Guyot

and telling her, bragging, about the meaning of the word according to the highest authorities of the time, Papa and Larousse.

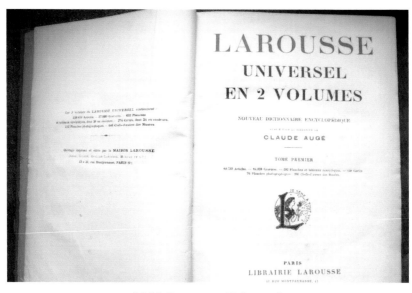

1929, Larousse Universel

Growing up, Larousse was our entertainment. Although we had a radio, a huge thing shaped like a gothic church, there were very few broadcasts and it was only turned on for news. In the evening my sister and I would look through the two tomes of illustrated Larousse, perusing through the colored plates of animals, paintings, costumes and industrial inventions. It made us dream of exotic places, things we did not know but knew existed elsewhere.

Laure Reichek née Guyot

1929, Larousse Universel

1929, Larousse Universel

Our grandfather had gone to Madagascar after the First World War to study tropical diseases, since many of our soldiers had come from the French colonies. He had seen some of the animals pictured in the Larousse and could vouch for their existence. We even could see the photo of Grandpa and Grandma in Tananarive. Africa was the most exotic place we knew of, and we invented games based on what we knew of the continent. We even pretended that our toy dog was a monkey and our small blue wooden elephant was roaming an equatorial forest on the floor of our bedroom. We made a tent with our bed sheet and chairs and called it our camp in the savannah. Oh, what a few pictures in a Larousse can do!

Laure Reichek née *Guyot*

Antecedents

Adjutor Marcoux was born in Canada, probably at the end of the 19th century. He came to France to visit the family of the man who had married his favorite daughter, Fernande, who was to become my mother several years later. Mr. Marcoux lived in Quebec with his family and had several other children there.

The year of his visit to Paris must have been between 1928 and 1930, the year of my birth. My parents lived on a barge on the Seine without water, electricity, or the advantages of a sewer system. My mother had been sent to France to pursue advanced musical studies but had instead married an artist-painter and lived happily and romantically, if uncomfortably, in a nonmoving sand barge moored at the foot of Notre-Dame. The barge had only one room from bow to stern and a roof of various leaky materials, later replaced by a proper enclosure with windows. It was towed to various quays around central Paris to comply with government regulations of river traffic, length of stays in one place, and mooring fees. My parents were very poor.

Nothing is known of Mr. Marcoux's visit to Paris. However, much is known of his visit to the small town in Berry where my future paternal grandparents lived. It was reported to me, many years after my birth, that this

Laure Reichek née Guyot

Canadian grandfather had left unforgettable memories in the town.

First, Marcoux was a giant of a man, wide, with lots of curly yellow hair and a very thick moustache. His behavior, however, was what impressed (some would say, scandalized) the inhabitants, who rarely saw a foreigner, especially one that size and with such comportment that could not be explained, since it had never been seen among folks who knew each other and each other's lineages going back centuries.

As a guest in my father's parents' house, he shocked everyone. Before meals, for example, he would go in the kitchen, lift the lids of every pot on the stove, and put a finger in each one and lick it. Then, having already made his choice, would refuse dishes presented to him at the table except the one to his liking, from which he would take enormous portions, leaving little for the others.

After lunch, he would walk the quarter-mile to the Café du Nord, where he would order "the whole shelf of liquors", drink them, and then stretch himself out on the red leather bench and go into such a deep sleep that he could not be awakened.

The only hotel in town, above the café, was also called Hotel du Nord. No one knew why it was named this, since our town was 350 kms south of Paris. Its

Laure Reichek née Guyot

original owners may have been from the North. But, such was its name.

It must have been a very primitive sort of hotel—there were very few travelers then. The hotel had electricity like the rest of the town but no running water and no sewer system. The toilet was in the yard, as was the pump over the well.

The hotel had a little bus, called an omnibus, to carry passengers and their luggage from the train station. It was entered from the rear and had two benches parallel to its walls. It took the bus driver and three men from the café—customers eager to assist in order to enter, probably for the first time, into my grandparents' house—to lift the huge sleeping man and carry him upstairs to his room.

The amount of alcohol consumed each day by Mr. Marcoux was phenomenal and gained him the admiration of Monsieur Dulac, the proprietor of the café, and the reprobation of some; but for the majority of the inhabitants, awe mingled with fear, as if a huge, brutish animal had suddenly appeared among them.

My paternal grandparents bore Mr. Marcoux's visit with grace, although I was told later that many of the handshakes they received during that time felt like the handshakes received at the cemetery after a funeral by the family of the deceased.

Laure Reichek née Guyot

When I was old enough to understand such things, perhaps around six or seven years old, after my mother's death, I was told of my maternal grandfather's visit. People in the town still talked about it as one of the unusual events that had happened in their lives, such as the day my father drove his motorcycle into the pharmacy at the angled intersection of the two roads in town to avoid a bus coming around the bend or the day the county's stallion bolted and dropped his uniformed rider in the midst of a wedding procession after being blinded by the phosphorous flash of the town photographer.

Mr. Marcoux's visit must not have been long, perhaps not a week but certainly at least five days, since it was the custom to entertain long-distance travelers for at least that many days.

One never knew whether Mr. Marcoux was in touch with my mother while she lived. After his visit, my paternal grandparents only heard of him once; after the Second World War, a Consulate in North Africa reported he had died there and had another wife but had left his estate to me, the daughter of his favorite daughter. My paternal grandparents, who had taken care of me since I was 11 days old, refused to make inquiries regarding the estate.

Perhaps their memories of my wild Canadian grandfather's visit had forever tainted any relationship

Laure Reichek née Guyot

they may have wished to have with a distant relative. One cannot choose one's ancestors, can one?

Children talk to each other and ask questions, mostly about their relatives. Everybody has relatives. Everyone knew the names of everyone else's parents and grandparents. They were usually visible and, when they were not, it was understood that they were in our cemetery or another one nearby.

No one was confused by the fact that I called my grandparents Papa and Maman. That was their role and that was accepted by all the other children— and their parents, too, who, when talking to my grandparents about me, said, "your daughter".

The problem was caused by the question: "Where are your grandparents?" I had trouble answering that, since most people in the village knew that my "parents" were really my grandparents, that my mother was dead, and that my father, if alive, was somewhere in IndoChina.

So, what do you answer when another eight-year-old asks you where are your grandparents?

Laure Reichek née Guyot

Accident
Chateaumeillant, Cher, France, 1937–1945

Although he lived for a couple of days in a coma after his accident, Monsieur Demenois did not survive the crash of his Rolls Royce in front of the castle in Culan. His chauffeur, Etienne Leblanc, did.

Rolls-Royce Phantom II

Other men had died there, in the deep ravine. Nothing very unusual about that. But a Rolls Royce had never been seen before. So the car was what people talked about. The beauty, the size, the comfort of the machine. Even as a wreck, it imposed awe. The vases of

Laure Reichek née Guyot

cut glass inside, between each door, had not even been broken. The white roses had fallen out, but the vases had remained affixed in their golden loops. Something worth talking about. Vases in a car! The local inhabitants had heard of or seen in magazines Delages, Talboots, or Delahayes, but an English car? Never.

As to Monsieur Demenois, it was quickly learned that he had been born in a small town south of Culan. His mother had been a servant in the small manor house of a local minor nobleman. The local farmers called the place "the Chateau," since it had a medieval tower on one side and was surrounded by a large forest. By local standards, it was an imposing structure with slate roofs and was impeccably maintained, yet it was a very unassuming, private place, as were most of the manors in Berry. From the main road, only the roofs and the top of the tower could be seen.

It had been assumed long ago that the child of Ninon Demenois had been fathered by the Viscount, and no one thought more about it. As a small child, Philippe Autissier grew up in the Chateau, among several other children belonging to the other servants and day laborers. His mother continued her work there, mostly as a cleaning woman.

At age six, Philippe was sent to boarding school in Chateauroux. He was a tall boy for his age, good looking, intelligent and disciplined. On holidays he would come

Laure Reichek née Guyot

back to visit his mother and play with his childhood friends. Although better dressed than his playmates, he never flaunted his advantages over the children of farmers or sharecroppers.

He was very affectionate with his mother. His unusual height, like that of the Viscount's, gave him a natural air of aloofness but not superiority. His mother, after all, was just a servant. When Philippe reached his twelfth birthday, the Viscount sent him to Paris to a boarding school where Latin and Greek were taught.

Philippe made a few trips from Paris to Culan to visit his mother before her death when he was 18. After receiving his baccalaureate, he continued his studies in Paris. His mother Ninon died sometime during the war. He was seen at the local cemetery, where she was buried in a simple grave with a small marble marker. After that, he was never seen again in the region.

The Viscount died 10 years later, and the Chateau was abandoned. It was sold to a local and is now the summer residence of an Englishman.

From Etienne Leblanc, we learned that Mr. Demenois was a very rich industrialist, that he was a widower, and that his destination was a small hamlet near the town of Chateauroux. News travels very quickly in small towns. There was no need for newspapers—few people read them at that time, and they were delivered by the local bus several days after the fact. Newspapers and

Laure Reichek née Guyot

magazines were dropped at the *papeterie,* the store where one could buy small books, postcards, notebooks and other school supplies, as well as candies.

A small notice, two lines in the obituary section, was printed the following week after Mr. Demenois's death. The notice mentioned he had been born and raised in the small town of Culan. By the time the notice was published, everybody already knew.

No one saw Philippe again until Leblanc revealed to the authorities, and therefore everybody, that Monsieur Demenois was a rich industrialist who had made a fortune in steel and that he was on his way to an isolated farm.

Solange, the name of a saint, is a very common name in Berry. History or legend, one or the other depending on your faith, says that such a person existed.

Solange Autissier, named after St Solange, was a very pretty girl and a very good, natural dancer. She was 17 when she met and fell in love with Phillippe Demenois at the local fair.

Six months after the death of Philippe Demenois, a Parisian lawyer arrived at the farm of Solange's daughter, Solangelette Autissier, to inform her that she was the legal and only heir to Mr. Demenois' fortune. It seems logical to assume that the 27-year-old farmer must have been surprised—or had her mother or her

mother's parents told her that her father was Philippe Demenois? We do not know.

Solangelette's mother and grandparents had died by that time, and she was running the small farm she had inherited from them. A mailman, retired because of injury to a leg, helped her run the farm. He lived in a nearby hamlet, and they planned to be married once the harvest was done. He was older than she but was a good, simple man, reliable and of clean habits. They intended to stay in the small, one-room farm with its stable, hay barn, outdoor well, and outhouse.

Etienne Leblanc received several fractures and a concussion. He remained many weeks in the hospital in St. Amand, and it is from him that we learned the story.

7. CULAN (Cher). — Vue Générale.

general view, Culan

Laure Reichek née *Guyot*

general view, Culan

Medieval chateau, Culan

viaduct and chateau, Culan

Medieval chateau, Culan

Laure Reichek née Guyot

viaducts, Culan

bridge and washerwoman, Culan

Laure Reichek née *Guyot*

The Compost Pit
Chateaumeillant, Cher, France, 1937–1945

It was the year of the Débacle.

The Maginot Line, thought impregnable, had not been breached. It had been bypassed.

The German Army had simply gone around it and was coming from the north. First, we saw French officers in cars driving south, then the foot soldiers, those who had gone to war with flowers in their guns to fight the war to end all wars, singing "Y'a Hitler sur la ligne Maginot." Now, the French army was walking it did not know where, heads down, eyes vacant, hungry, dirty, stinking, dragging itself like mangy dogs, begging

Bundesarchiv, Bild 101I-055-1592-05A

retreating French army, La Deroute

Laure Reichek née Guyot

for food and water, hugging walls in case of enemy air attacks.

We watched, as stunned as they.

Our courtyard was full of soldiers, washing at our water pump, eating all of Grandma's canned fruit and vegetables brought up from the cellar.

All the yards were full of the remnants of an army. When they moved on, they would be replaced by more of the same. For many days, on and on went this disorganized parade of shuffling, creeping, wounded men, called "La Déroute".

One day, as I was taking food in a small metal pail from my grandparents' house to my great-grandmother's for her dog—just stale bread soaked in the hot water we poured over the plates before washing them, just to give the bread a little taste—it was snatched from my hands by a hungry soldier. I kept saying, "But it's for the dog!" and the soldier had replied, "But I'm hungry too." I was shocked—shaken and deep down humiliated by the sight of a man gulping down dog soup without a spoon.

Then, one day, the *defilé* stopped. There were no more men. Where did all these poor men go?

The larger town—where I had been in boarding school, since our village only had a primary school—had been bombed, so I had been brought back to attend the small girls' school and given additional tutors for

Laure Reichek née *Guyot*

subjects not taught there. The village—a small town, just under 1900 inhabitants—also had a boys' school at the other end of town. Some of the children came to school every day from isolated farms or hamlets after a one- or two-hour walk, most in wooden clogs without socks. In wintertime, some put straw in their clogs to keep warm and carried a hot brick wrapped in a towel against their chests. Lucky ones had heavy hand-knit socks, caps, and mittens.

No one ever complained because that was the way it was and could not be changed. In springtime, children would come to school with great bouquets of wildflowers—primroses (called coucous), peri-winkles, and violets—that we copied in "art" class.

We did not look down on the poorly dressed and shod children who sat next to us town children because there was some sort of awe in front of their unstated stamina, dogged perseverance, the straightforward demand for equal treatment in their eyes. They did every day tasks we could not imagine, we town softies. Besides, some of them had shown themselves to be our equals in intelligence.

Some of these children really smelled very badly of cow manure and other potent odors, but we accepted that, along with the smell of chalk and ink permeating the classrooms. Even dirty children do not smell as bad as unwashed adults. Children do not perspire as much,

Laure Reichek née Guyot

I guess. Or because they do not drink wine as much as grownups.

We did drink a little wine with our meals, and, in wintertime, coming home from school half frozen, we were given a big bowl of half wine-half water, warm, with sugar and spices. That did not prevent the chilblains that we had on knuckles and knees, but it did warm your chest—the most important part of the body, we knew—for a few hours, enough time to do your homework. War or no war, heat in the house or not, enough food or not, enough light or not, there was always homework and wine.

Wine was more common and plentiful than food; everyone knew how to make it, and the vineyards

LE SANCERROIS   Chavignol-sous-Sancerre Cher) — Les Vendanges

the grape harvest, Chavignol-sous-Sancerre

Laure Reichek née *Guyot*

always produced grapes, sometimes more, sometimes less, but always enough.

pickers

returning from the harvest

Laure Reichek née *Guyot*

There was to be a math test. I did not like math, pretty close to hated it. I was not good at it. It was too dry for my taste, and you had to write down all the theorems learned by rote in the left-hand margin of your geometry problems. Even one word left out was counted as a mistake.

So, to avoid taking the test, I came up with the idea of breaking a leg. Grandpa, the doctor, would have to put my leg in a cast and probably make me rest a few days in bed, as he recommended with broken limbs. If I did not manage to break a leg, I might break an arm—the right one, preferably, since I was right-handed—or had been made to be, since left-handedness was not acceptable then.

No problem. We had, in a corner of the garden, a large compost pit. It was made of cement, about eight feet long and five feet wide. In it, Eugene, the gardener and my grandfather's orderly since the First World War, threw the manure from our chicken coop and rabbit hutches, as well as all the debris from the garden and the kitchen.

I conceived the idea of jumping from one end of the compost wall to the other. I was very agile, but this was a long leap to make, so surely I would hit the opposite wall with one part of my body or another. Before going to school, the day of the exam, I went to the garden, with

Laure Reichek née Guyot

determination and sure of success, and after pumping my legs as before a sprint, leaped off the cement wall.

I did hit the wall—a little—but only with my forehead and fell inside the warm composted manure. I must have screamed, unbeknownst to me, because Eugene and his wife Suzanne, who helped Grandma with the housework, came running and yelling, "Look what she has done now!"

I was carried into the house, washed, re-clothed, and brought to my grandfather's surgery room where, without a word, my forehead was painted with a burning iodine, then bandaged. By now, I had a bump the size of half a grapefruit but no broken bones.

I was ashamed, embarrassed by my stupidity, and worried about what would happen next.

With his pale blue eyes burning into mine, Grandpa just said, "No harm done. Don't you have an exam today, young lady?"

And that was that. Feeling defeated, like those soldiers in Déroute, I went to school with a pain in my head, a bandage on my forehead, and my pride, situated somewhere in my midsection, churning.

Laure Reichek née Guyot

The Slap
Chateaumeillant, Cher, France, 1937–1945

It was the summer of '41. The town where I was in boarding school (I had been in boarding school since the age of six) had been bombed, so I had returned to my grandparents' village. My grandfather had found tutors—Monsieur Fradet for Latin and Mlle Perronet for English and French.

I now know that Mlle Perronet, a retired grammar school teacher, did not know English well, but I liked going to her house, which she shared with another retired teacher, Mlle Fusibet. I had heard deprecating rumors about these women and had told Grandpa, who had replied that these ladies were honorable and their lifestyle was nobody's business. Mlle Perronet could play the piano (a little) and managed to teach me "Ba Ba Black Sheep" and "Oranges and Lemons" over the course of the summer. Mlle Fusibet tended the large garden, where we would often walk, dictionary in hand, to learn the English names of plants. But we never made a sentence with them, so I always forgot them.

Monsieur Fradet lived on the outskirts of the village at the top of a very steep hill. His house was surrounded by his small vineyard, kept in weedless condition. He taught me Latin, gave me lessons, and made me recite my verbs and declinations.

Laure Reichek née Guyot

I did not like going to Monsieur Fradet's house. The hill was so steep I had to dismount my bicycle before reaching the top, out of breath—bicycles had only one gear then. My lessons were in mid-afternoon when the heat was at its worst.

That afternoon I had gone to a small meadow on the outskirts where we kept Ponette, the horse that drew my grandfather's buggy, since there was no gasoline for his car. I knew daisies grew in the ditch by the hedgerow. Also, honeysuckle and blackberries.

No one in town had a wristwatch. A few men, like my grandfather, had pocket watches at the end of chains tied to the buttonhole of their vests and kept in a pocket. The town hall had a very big clock that struck the hours, the quarters, and the halves. It could be heard everywhere, and I heard it strike three. Time to go back home, mount my bicycle, and go to my lesson. But I was having such a good time and was carrying an armload of daisies. And it was cool in the ditch.

The idea occurred to me to pretend that I did not hear the clock. Grandpa was rarely home during the day, going on his errands to take care of his patients and returning only at the end of the day for dinner.

I stayed in the meadow and returned only around four for the *goûter,* the four o'clock snack. The front door was, in fact, two, joined by a large metal bar with a sculpted knob in the middle. When both sides were

Laure Reichek née Guyot

opened, you could bring in a stretcher. I came in with my flowers only to see Grandpa coming toward me in the corridor.

"Where have you been? Don't you have a lesson with Monsieur Fradet? Don't you know the time?"

"No," I said.

Instinctively, I backed up against the door, guilt rising from my feet, paralyzing me on the spot where my back touched the door and the left side of my head touched the metal doorknob. I could easily see that Grandpa was furious. His voice was angry, loud, uncontrolled. It was so unlike him, and I could not imagine what the fuss was about. But guilty I was. Before I knew what to think, he was hitting me in the face. The left side of my face hit the doorknob several times. He would not stop. After the initial surprise at the depth of his anger, my head began to hurt and I could feel blood running down my face and into my collar. I must have been screaming for Grandma, and Suzanne, the maid, appeared, yelling, "Stop, stop, you're going to kill her!" I just stood there, crying, in pain, feeling the blood running from my temple to my neck. I thought perhaps I would die. Wished I would. It would serve him right. When he finally stopped, his anger exhausted, all he said was, "Take her to surgery."

I was carried, dragged, escorted by the two women and made to sit on a stool next to the operating table.

Laure Reichek née Guyot

The wound was cleaned and dressed, no stitches. And I now had a bandage around my head.

After all that was necessary was done, Grandpa said: "Now go to Mr. Fradet and apologize."

I was speechless. My head throbbed. It was still hot, and I was not thinking of the fact that I would miss my goûter too, but I dared not disobey Grandpa.

Angry, ashamed, hurt, with Grandpa, Grandma, and Suzanne watching me, I mounted my bicycle, left the house and rode in the direction of Mr. Fradet's house, up that stiff hill.

I was stunned. Stunned by the depth and ferocity of Grandpa's anger. "Why? Why?" I kept asking myself. Sure, I had lied. I knew the time, had heard the clock. But he had never slapped me before on the face. Occasionally, Grandpa had hit me on the buttocks, but usually I was given a lecture, his eyes piercing me like lances, and that was all.

Like the time I had been caught by Eugene trying to drag a ladder from the garage to get to the roof after having seen a picture of a parachute. The intention had been to put the ladder against the wall of the woodshed, climb up with an umbrella, and jump down with the umbrella opened. All the ladders were made of wood then and were very heavy, so I had not gone very far when Eugene, grandpa's orderly/aide/gardener and Suzanne's husband, met me and asked me what I

Laure Reichek née Guyot

thought I was doing. Proud of myself and my knowledge, I told him my intentions, and, of course, he in turn told Grandpa. That fostered a long lesson on gravity, the speed of falling objects, etc., etc., and a spanking on the buttocks to add weight to the discussion lest I forget.

Eugene and Suzanne had the right to discipline me whenever they felt I needed it, which was quite often. I was very mischievous, although I thought at the time "adventurous" a better description of myself.

They kept a cat-o'-nine-tails whip in the kitchen, where one or the other could find it most of the time. The whip had a wooden handle and a dozen or so, maybe nine, long leather straps, about an inch wide.

It was kept on top of the hutch, so I could not reach it even if I stood on a chair (I tried). It stung when it hit your calves, but Eugene or Suzanne never hit very hard, although it left marks on your skin for a couple of days. Of course, in those days girls never ever wore pants, even when there was a foot of snow on the ground. Pants on women led to lewd behavior, smoking, driving cars, and, inevitably, to immoral conduct (meaning fornication outside of wedlock). It seemed that every sin led to fornication, the ultimate, unforgiveable offense with the worst consequences now and in the hereafter.

I made it up the hill and arrived at Mr. Fradet's house to find him in his vineyard, a copper sprayer strapped to his back. He saw me and my bandage and asked what

Laure Reichek née Guyot

happened. Was I going to tell him that I had gotten the beating of my life for having tried to avoid coming to my lesson? No, no, no. So, I lied again and answered that I had fallen off my bike, all the time trying to imagine whether Grandpa could possibly know what I had just said.

Mr. Fradet then told me that it was too late for my lesson, that he had to continue what he was doing because the sprayer tank was almost full and he had to finish it lest it thicken and clog the sprayer line. I should go home and enjoy myself.

I was furious. I could feel my veins engorge with blood. The pain in my head was knocking so hard behind my eyeballs that my pupils were out of focus. Now I knew what "seeing red" was. I had gone to all this trouble, pain, effort to get here, and the old man did not even care. I had been made to feel guilty for nothing. That was not fair. That was not just. That was not human. That was not....

Coming back down the hill, coasting, had always been a pleasure. The air in your hair made you feel a little bit like those aviators who did tricks with their machines at the air show in Chateauroux, the big town 46 km away. Or you could soar like the geese that flew twice a year above the town on their migrations to far away countries, even continents, across the Mediterranean Sea to Africa. The thought, as well as the physical contact with rushing air, gave you goose pimples, cleared the

Laure Reichek née Guyot

acid juices out of your stomach and the tangled wiring in your brain.

Why had Grandpa done this? He was neither an impulsive nor a violent man.

As I was free-falling down Main St., known as the Grande Rue, the only "rue" in fact, I began to put the elements of my misfortune together:

First—Your word is your word. You say you are going to do something? You do it.

Second—You do not lie to Grandpa. He knows when you are lying, as when you said you did not know what time it was.

Third—Mr. Fradet is as old as Grandpa. You respect your elders, no matter what. If an elder expects you, you go. He may also need the money he receives for teaching you.

Fourth—I have the same name as Grandpa. The family's name, honor, reputation, were at stake. Can't sully that.

I was rearranging, analyzing the arguments, asking questions and giving answers as Grandpa had taught me to do, riding at full speed back towards home. Before I entered the courtyard, I had my answers. Grandma greeted me with a tall, cool glass of lemonade and an aspirin. I knew that I was already forgiven. The lesson, however, still echoes 80 years later.

Laure Reichek née Guyot

Mr. Sotton

Chateaumeillant, Cher, France, 1937–1945

I do not know whether I could find the way to Mr. Sotton's house in the forest. I had never gone there by myself. I was a child then. But I would like to think that if someone pointed me in the right direction I would find my way. The way birds do. First the small dirt road, on the right it was, in the middle of the forest. Then perhaps a mile farther in, with ditches on both sides, the ground uneven, you suddenly came to a clearing. And there it was on the right, in the center of the open space.

A square house made of stone with two steps in front. Inside, just one room. A chimney, a table and two benches, a bed, and an armoire. Just one room, almost square, with only two windows, one on each side of the door. There was no electricity, no running water; the well was outside in front of the house. On the left side of the clearing was a large barn, larger than the house, with a stable for a horse and a wagon.

To the left of the door to the house was a small plank supported by rough wooden legs, on which stood a basin, pitcher, and a cake of soap. On the wall had been nailed a broken piece of mirror. This is where Monsieur Sotton washed and shaved. Although he had a thick grey moustache, the rest of his face was clean shaven. And that is where I saw a man shave himself for the first

Laure Reichek née *Guyot*

time. A man without a shirt, with suspenders dangling to his sides.

My grandfather used to be shaved twice a week by the village barber, who would come to the house and use a folding, long-blade razor he kept sharp by rubbing on a long leather strap attached to a chair. My grandfather's shirt would be covered by a large towel, and a round china basin with an indentation for the neck on one side would be placed under his chin, to receive soap and water.

Not so with Mr. Sotton. After soaping his face, he used a small-handled razor that he himself ran up and down his cheeks and neck. When finished, he simply splashed more water on his face, then threw the soapy water on the ground.

I was spellbound and fascinated and realized that the whole experience, due to the simplicity of the house and to the act of shaving alone, outside, in the middle of the forest, bare to the waist, was something more natural, more elemental than the same function performed in a bourgeois household such as ours. We had many rooms in our house: living room/dining-room, kitchen, offices, waiting room for my grandfather's patients, bedrooms, bathrooms, corridors, inside stairs and balconies and, outside, garage and sheds.

Here, at Mr. Sotton's, everything was compact, reduced, distilled, minimalized. It was not a house but

Laure Reichek née Guyot

a refuge against the elements. Its solidity exuded safety, tranquility. And then it occurred to me that Mr. Sotton's house was like his torso—strong, square, straight; not lean, yet with no extra fat; and of a color acquired by outdoor work, often in the sun without a shirt. The house may not have been comfortable by town standards, but it made you feel comfortable, at ease.

The space told you, *faites comme chez vous.*

There were no restrictions here, nothing to watch out for as in the houses of the village ladies my grandmother went to visit. In those houses, I had to stay still in my chair while the two women chatted about things I did not understand or was not interested in. I was warned in advance to watch where I put my feet (not on the chair rungs), not to touch anything, and not to squirm in my seat. My eyes would occupy the time looking at the objects on the mantelpiece—the clock, the shells from First World War cannons, the photograph of a deceased man in uniform. Mme Garnier's husband?

Laure Reichek née Guyot

Laure Reichek née *Guyot*

Docteur Guyot with his Croix de Guerre with bronze star

I had never been told whether she had been married. She had always looked like a widow to me. But why have shell casings on the mantelpiece? They were not pretty objects. They must be souvenirs, I thought then— souvenirs to remember the war. People were always talking about the war; veterans like my grandfather were everywhere. The "Great War" they called it, and yet my grandfather always talked about the horrors of it. The mud in the trenches, the stench, the lice, the lack of medicine, the horrible wounds from shells. A souvenir? A reminder of some event, someone?

Sometimes, if I were lucky, there would be a painting or a reproduction of one, a seascape, a landscape, something to get lost in until the visit was over. At the house of Mme Garnier, I was given a cherry with stem, marinated in alcohol with sugar in a pretty little glass. I enjoyed that but at other houses, I was bored.

Here at Monsieur Sotton's, there was no boredom possible. There was too much to be seen, heard, smelled. The comfort was overwhelming, like being wrapped in a big comforter. No pretense—it was just itself. You did not have to say, "May I?" before sitting down. You just did what the others did: swing one leg over the bench, then the other. And there you were with your elbows on the table, something you would never do at home. And it felt good.

Laure Reichek née Guyot

His house looked like him, and he looked like his house. They suited each other, were an extension of each other.

When Mr. Sotton had finished shaving, he slipped his suspenders back on his shoulders, and we all went in to have a glass of wine, mine mixed with water. We sat on the benches on each side of a long, rough-hewn table, Mr. Sotton, my father and me, and the friend who had driven us there in a car. My father made the arrangements with Mr. Sotton for the use of his barn, where my father, a painter, wanted to do some large paintings. A small bed would be installed in a corner of the barn, next to the horse stall for warmth. That was all. My father would share Mr. Sotton's food.

Mr. Sotton was the forest keeper, the warden. His responsibilities were to keep the forest healthy and keep away poachers, clear dead trees, and maintain the road. He was allowed to kill all the game he could eat, gather all the mushrooms and plants he needed, and sell the cut dead wood.

After my mother's death when I was six, my father had felt the need to isolate himself to heal his pain. My grandfather had known Mr. Sotton and his wife before he became a widower and had attended Mme Sotton in her terminal illness. He knew of the peaceful existence of the forest keeper, his gentle straightforwardness.

Laure Reichek née Guyot

My father spent several springs and summers there, visibly healing his mind and body.

My grandfather and I, who lived half an hour away, would often go to visit. Mr. Sotton had a cocker spaniel by the name of Taillaut, which is the first word, the rallying call, before the hunt. The dog was as gentle as his master, and it was a pleasure to play with him. There was also an owl, without a name, that stood perched on a small gate closing the path to a pond. The bird just stood there, waiting for Mr. Sotton to bring bits of meat. I was fascinated by the way it moved its head from side to side, pivoting half a turn on its neck. Although its eyes were enormous, I was told that it could not see well in the daytime. It also had a strange smell, not pleasant. It was free to roam at night but simply chose to spend its day there on the gate, waiting for Monsieur Sotton's offerings.

On May Day, the holiday honoring working people, the custom was to go in the forests to gather lilies of the valley, in bloom at that time. It was an outing of mostly young people, the lily of the valley being associated with courtship. Girls and young women went in groups. Anything else would have been regarded as too "forward", unbecoming. Young men also went in groups. It was an occasion to meet *par hasard,* to check each other out. An occasion to say next time one met, "Oh, I saw you in the forest, remember me?"

Laure Reichek née Guyot

For days afterwards, the schoolteachers' desks would hold many bouquets of lily of the valley in glass jars, and the room traded its usual smell of chalk, erasers, and needing-to-be-washed clothes for the sweet smell of the little white bells. Enough to make you dream of the forest and the people you had seen there. Some, especially.

Then, Chateaumeillant was already a place young people wanted to run away from. Dull, boring, nothing changed in two hundred years. Nothing to do in one's spare time. But it was a place where older people who had gone to live in cities wanted to return to. For the peace and quiet, the soft look of its rounded hills, its small hamlets, unchanged in two hundred years.

For the young, there was no sense of privacy. Everyone knew everyone else, what they did—or were supposed to be doing—where and at what time. Any change in schedules or places was immediately noted and broadcast. "Where do you think she could have been going at this hour?", one neighbor would ask another. The question would make the rounds of the small town until a logical, plausible answer was found. And if not? Well, young people will be young people. Remember? And you wondered who she was going to meet at this hour and where.

The "where" was often the banks of the lake-pond-swamp, called the *étang* because it did not run all year.

Laure Reichek née Guyot

It was a very large pond formed by the damming of a swamp. On the dam, passed a road. One side of the road, opposite the pond, was much lower than the water side, and a small house of stone had been built there for the man who controlled the metal gates and sluice that maintained the water level. Farmers would back up their oxen-driven carts into the pond to fill barrels with water to irrigate their fields.

One could walk around half the pond and lie in the grass under huge poplars. The opposite half was lined by a dozen small houses. One could also walk toward the water source, about a mile, and find oneself on a narrow path with the waters clogged by water lilies and reeds on one side and high hedgerows of blackberry and honeysuckle on the other.

étang, Berry, Cher, France

Laure Reichek née Guyot

Once in a while, there would be a man fishing but only in the deeper part of the lake and there was no reason to go up a path that led nowhere. Unless, of course, you would have been the one embarrassed if you had gone there to spy. Therefore, it was a logical place for lovers to go—a safe place, since one couple was not likely to report on another.

Still, it would have been nice to have a private life, to have been able to go unnoticed anywhere, to wear clothes of one's choice, to fix one's hair as one pleased, to know that there were more movies than once a week. In proper theatres, too—not in the back room of a café, full of smoke, with an old projector that broke the film several times each time it was used, and where you had to go accompanied by a parent or another adult the way you did when there was a dance, in the same café, in the same room that had been transformed into a dance floor by applying wax shavings from an old candle to make it slippery.

There was a fee to be paid to enter the dance, since it had a live orchestra. An accordion, a drummer, and a saxophone usually made up the band that played polkas, waltzes and passo-dobles (a form of simplified tango), sometimes a fox-trot. There were no windows in that back room, only a door that was kept open for the heat that quickly became intense. The smell of body heat, added to the odor of clothing impregnated with the

Laure Reichek née Guyot

scents of cows, milk, hay, tobacco, was as intoxicating as the sweating hand of your dance partner on your back.

Marie-Rose and I watched through the open door, fascinated, studying the dancers' steps and moves. We were quite conscious of our peeping, of our emotions. Peeping, like eavesdropping, was strictly taboo, but peering into a public place was tolerated (after all the door was open), provided that you did not stay too long. Time and place was everything, and they always came together in acceptable or objectionable fashion.

Here, at the door of the café, glaring, probably with our mouths open, it was like looking at that Japanese fan my grandfather had bought for my grandmother on one of his trips to Bourges, the largest town in Berry. On the fan, an artist had painted the scene of people having tea, seen through the clouds of cherry trees in bloom. The eye would penetrate the branches to partially—only partially—reveal what the persons in the bungalow were doing. There was mystery there, the fascination of discovery. On the dance floor, it was to discover what kind of shoes the dancers were wearing, what kind of clothes. Slowly putting together the elements of what looked like pleasure. Adding up the pieces of the puzzle that constituted that desirable picture of dancing couples.

When I was finally allowed to go in at age fifteen (with my grandmother on a bench on the sidelines), my

Laure Reichek née Guyot

early impression of Paradise was confirmed. Since I was a good dancer, I rarely had a rest and my grandmother enjoyed herself, too, watching me dancing correctly, the way she had taught me in the kitchen since I was five years old, standing on her feet, holding her by her lowered arms while she sang some tune from 1900.

Men and women who did not need chaperones would often disappear from the dance floor, and everyone would know what it meant, talk about it, assess the prospects of a lasting relationship, point to the good and bad points of each partner, agree or disagree on imagined possible future developments. Most people did not have time to read books or newspapers. We were our own tabloids.

After the war, running water and sewers were installed in the whole town and its nearest farms. Many older people who had gone, years before, to work in larger cities, returned. They bought old houses and remodeled them, installing "modern" kitchens and bathrooms. Automobiles appeared. Every house had a car; every farm, a truck, tractor, machines to separate the cream from the milk, butane stoves. Farming methods changed. Hedgerows were removed, old trees uprooted, land flattened to enlarge fields and make them smooth for tractors and harvesters, ancient stone houses destroyed.

Laure Reichek née Guyot

Some places do remain the way they were two hundred years ago. They are known to those who were born earlier or lived in the area. Others have become tourist attractions, beautiful places to visit-under supervision—with large parking lots for buses and cars, sometimes with hotels and inns nearby.

Monsieur Sotton has been dead for more than half a century, but I have been told that his house is still there in that clearing in the forest. Someone probably lives there today.

But I will not disturb the new occupants, nor will I try to peek, even if I could find the way.

The memory of the place, the man who lived there more than 70 years ago, must remain safe.

Laure Reichek née Guyot

The Old Woman and a Goat

Chateaumeillant, Cher, France, 1937–1945

When I was a child and asked what I wanted to be when I grew up, I would reply, "An old woman with a goat". Everyone thought that to be a sensible answer.

In Berry before WW II, there were many old women who knitted woolen socks for sale. They were often seen sitting in ditches while their goat, tethered to their leg by a rope, browsed in the hedgerows of blackberries and honeysuckle. That way the hedgerows were trimmed and the goats fed. One woman, Madame Chirade, was the one who sold my family our winter socks, and we knew her well. Madame Chirade would come to our house to take our measurements once a year. She carried no tape or other instrument. Instead, she used a string with a knot at one end and wrapped it around our closed fist; she would make another knot where the two ends of the string met. Apparently, the circumference of a fist is equal to the length of the owner's foot. That fascinated me and was part of the reason why I wanted to grow up to do that. But the other reason, the main one, no doubt, was the goat. I loved goats and dogs. There are lots of goats in Berry. Their milk makes many cheeses famous. Valencay, Crotins de Chavignolles, and hundreds of others that are sold on market days in every village or small town.

Laure Reichek née *Guyot*

54 - St-AMAND-MONTROND (CHER) - PAYSANNES BERRICHONNES AU MARCHÉ

peasant woman at market, St-Amand-Montrond

Place du Marché, La Châtre

Now, for genealogy. Papa, who was really my grandfather, was my biological father's father. Mama, who was really my grandmother, was my father's mother. I had lived with them, exclusively, since I was 11 days old.

My real father and mother, at the time of my birth, were living on a barge on the Seine in Paris. My father was a painter, which had been accepted by his parents after several known artists were consulted and had declared that my father had talent.

The problem was the *péniche* (barge), *The Bucanier*— no electricity, no running water, no heat, no sewer. That was too much for my bourgeois grandparents (grandpa

Laure Reichek née Guyot

was a doctor). They were convinced I would die in that environment, so I was taken away without discussion. The fact that my mother was a foreigner, a Canadian Native American, must have played a role in the decision. But I think that the most important, of course unstated, factor was that grandma had had only one child (my father) and wanted another.

**St. Maur (Laure's father) on The Bucanier,
moored on the Seine in Paris**

Laure Reichek née Guyot

Laure with Grandmother-Mama

Grandpa had been born into the bourgeoisie. His father had also been a doctor. But Grandma was the daughter of a very poor railroad worker with nine children. On his walk in his native city of Montluçon, Grandpa had seen his future wife on the threshold of her tenement building, falling in love on the spot. The two eloped to Bordeaux, where he finished his medical school and my real father was born.

Laure Reichek née *Guyot*

I had been told who my real parents were; I found the thought interesting but had only love and affection for my surrogate ones. They loved me, and I loved them. No one in the town ever referred to them as my grandparents. It was always: "Marinette, go home, your mama wants you," or "Where's your father today?"

Laure's grandmother in her living room

Laure Reichek née Guyot

Rainulfe and Solange

Chateaumeillant, Cher, France, 1937–1945

In the 19th and 20th centuries, many Berichons named their daughters Solange after the 9th century martyr and saint. In 1877, a small pamphlet had just been written by L'Abbé Joseph Bernard on the life of the young shepherdess killed by a young nobleman, named Rainulfe, for refusing his advances.

According to the Abbé Bernard, the young woman, from a very pious, poor family, was grazing her sheep near St. Martin d'Aubigny when a young man on his horse came upon her and was stricken by her beauty, her innocence and grace. Solange told Rainulfe that she was wedded to God and could not answer his demands. The nobleman returned to the fields where her sheep grazed, each time pleading with her to accede to his love, finally offered to marry her, to share his castle and wealth. Solange did not yield and always answered the same way, "I am married to God and, therefore, cannot marry you."

On the 10th of May, 880, enraged, Rainulfe took out his sword and severed her head. According to Abbé Bernard and the legend that followed, she picked up her head, carried it in her arms and dropped it in the nearby fountain, while saying, "Jesus, my spouse, here I come."

Laure Reichek née Guyot

Today, on that spot, stands a sculpture of Solange, as well as a small chapel, visited each year by thousands of pilgrims, mostly of Portuguese origin, who may have conflated the legend of Solange, who was canonized by the Church, with that of Our Lady of Fatima. The sculpture shows a young woman without a head, with a sheep also with severed legs, at her left.

The legend survives and is believed by many Catholics. Many believers still name their daughters Solange. The writer George Sand, who wrote many books on the lives and beliefs of pre-industrial Berry, also named her daughter Solange. George Sand's manor and hamlet at Nohant are still standing and receive many thousands of visitors each year.

Sainte-Solange—La Chapelle

Bigoudi

Chateaumeillant, Cher, France, 1937-1945

Some of the older folks in the village may have known his name. To everyone else, he was Bigoudi, meaning "hair curler"—a joke, perhaps, since he was bald, although he always wore an old cap. Or he may have had a full head of curls when he was young. When we knew him, he was of indescribable age. But old.

He was small, very thin, sun-tanned, had no glasses and no teeth. He wore the kind of jacket and trousers that all workmen and farmers wore, made of a royal blue, heavy cotton that used to be made in the town of Nimes in the south of France—hence, denim in English. Except that Bigoudi's suit was no longer blue. It had become grey with a hint of pale blue—an optimistic sort of grey, not the sad, pale, mouse grey that children in mourning had to wear for a year. The black mourning clothes of an adult were, perhaps, considered too harsh for children, too sad, too painful.

He was the town crier; in those days, few had radios. He went from farm to farm on an abandoned grey bicycle, bringing news from town hall about electoral campaigns; agricultural association meetings; news of births, deaths, marriages; gossip. On his back, Bigoudi carried a small drum attached like a knapsack by two straps, and he kept two small sticks in his jacket

Laure Reichek née Guyot

pocket (along with his tin of bicarbonate of soda). Upon arriving in a neighborhood, he would dismount, drop his bicycle on the ground, take his drum and sticks, and beat a roll—the kind to signify attention—hear ye, hear ye. After several doors or windows had opened, he would take out the notice in his breast pocket and read, slowly but loudly. His speech lacked clear Ts and Ds, but it was understood.

Bigoudi was also the town alcoholic. In every farm he visited, he was given a glass of our local wine for his effort—having pedaled miles up and down hills and valleys on his old bicycle without gears. We did not make fun of Bigoudi, as we would of other drunks, the kind that staggered from the cafés after market on Friday afternoons, who yelled at their horses and sometimes beat them. Bigoudi never yelled, never insulted anyone. His alcoholism was his disease, like the tuberculosis affecting so many persons in our area. He was our crier first; his alcoholism was his affliction and did not change our opinion of him as a good man.

He carried in his jacket pocket a tin can of bicarbonate of soda from which he took a good mouthful after each drink. Our local wine is called vin gris. It is a very acidic white wine made from the Pinot Noir variety of grapes. The skin of the fruit is dark blue, but its flesh is pale green. The wine is drunk as cool as possible. In the times of Bigoudi, no one had refrigerators, so it was brought up from the cool cellar before drinking or put

Laure Reichek née Guyot

in a pail down into the well. It was consumed mostly in summertime and was tart and refreshing. Also, very cheap. It flowed on Friday afternoons at the end of our market days. Many cafés only existed in the kitchens of people who owned a vineyard or in the kitchens of their relatives.

The press belonged to a cooperative of small growers, and it would move from neighborhood to neighborhood at "crushing" time. It was a small wooden press, the screw hand-carved from a tree trunk, usually walnut in our area. Men took turns in turning the press mounted on the back of a wooden flat-bed chariot. The raw wine—really, grape juice—came down via a small gutter protruding from the trough under the screw, directly into a huge large bottle covered with wicker in the form of a basket, easy to transport to the farm, where the juice would go slowly through its fermentation process. Barrels were sterilized by burning sulfur sticks inside, slowly removing the oxygen and, therefore, all aerobic bacteria. The yellow sticks of sulfur were held in suspension by a large, deep, spoon-like piece of metal, whose handle reached outside the barrel where it was fastened, a cork and cloth making the barrel absolutely airtight.

Laure Reichek née Guyot

portable grape press

at the wine press, Sancerre

Laure Reichek née *Guyot*

Photo A. Joulin, Valençay (Indre)
501 - LA VERNELLE (Indre) — Préparation aux Vendanges

barrel repair in preparation for the harvest

After the grape pressing was done and the juice sent to its journey before becoming wine, a lot of residue—skins, stems—were left in the trough under the screw. This unfermented residue was taken to the *alambic*—the still—to be transformed into *eau de vie de marc.* We children would go to look at the beautiful machine, all brass and copper, a long, horizontal cylinder with a burner being constantly stoked with wood. It looked like the front end of a locomotive, smoking, hot, shaking on its wheels, all of it immaculately shining. On top was a long, spiraling glass tube, at the end of which the raw alcohol dripped slowly into glass bottles. This was the *eau de vie de marc,* rare, precious, to bring the sick back to health.

Laure Reichek née *Guyot*

Edit. Corset.

Chabris. — Distillateur ambulant

mobile distillery

Eugene, my grandfather's orderly and gardener, would tie a bottle, carefully set on a little wooden platform in a pear tree so as to enclose a just-forming pear. The pear would slowly grow inside the bottle and, when matured, fall to the bottom of the bottle. You had then a fully grown pear inside a bottle, puzzling many visitors who did not understand how you could put a large pear into a small-necked bottle.

At the end of a day's work, Bigouti was often found asleep in a ditch, his bicycle lying down on an abutment. Passing carriages would pick him up and carry him and his bicycle back to his house. If no one came, he just slept there. Bigoudi lived in the oldest part of the village known as the *faubourg*, a series of small stone houses set side by side, each with only one door and

Laure Reichek née *Guyot*

one window. There was no electricity, no sewers, and no water available except at a public pump a few hundred yards away.

In his unique position, wandering from farm to farm, he encountered abandoned wheels, tires, metal objects, etc.... Bigoudi was a collector, and his house was said to be a real dump, which we did not doubt, since he always wore the same dirty old clothes, summer and winter.

A few days after the Allies landed in Normandy, everyone in the village assumed that the war would soon be over. We all had visions of American, English, Polish, Canadian soldiers parading through our villages and towns. Under the direction of Mademoiselle Limousin, a retired school teacher, we learned to sing "God Save the King," which was the only song in English she knew. Looking through our old Larousse dictionary (edition 1929), we found pictures of flags from every country. We were put to work painting flags to string across the main street when the Allies came marching in. America was to us the land of plenty—plenty of soldiers, plenty of tanks and guns, planes, ships, food, and liberty for all. We could not wait to receive the liberators, and we strung up our line of paper flags (double-faced) across the road.

The liberators did not arrive when expected. From the few radios, illegally kept from the authorities who had confiscated most of them, we knew that the Allies

Laure Reichek née Guyot

were encountering fierce resistance and huge casualties in Normandy.

It was Bigoudi who rushed into my grandfather's consulting room to say that a German column was coming our way and we had better take those flags down if we did not want to all be vaporized by guns and flame-throwers.

One end of the rope was attached to the stove in my upstairs bedroom and the other to Monsieur Thevenin's house across the street. Eugene was sent to untie the ropes and bring down the flags. Eugene had been in the trenches with Grandpa in the First World War and had come back to live in our town. He helped in surgery, processed the x-rays, took care of the car and the garden, cleaned the fireplaces, the gutters, the courtyard, while his wife Suzanne worked with my grandmother in the house, cleaning, cooking, giving me my weekly bath. They lived in a small house with a big garden on the outskirts of town. They came to work in our house every day except Sunday. They had no children. Suzanne had had tuberculosis and my grandfather had advised against parenthood, but they had been given, or taken, the right to treat me as their daughter, and they were the ones who generally punished me when I had done something wrong. They kept a cat-o'-nine-tails whip in the kitchen that they used often on my legs—gently. I knew that they loved me, and I loved them as another set of relatives.

Laure Reichek née Guyot

Earlier on I had learned that they had the right to discipline me. Eugene had given me quite a verbal and physical lashing after I had snapped the heads off all the tulips in the flower garden—just to hear the crack, the exciting sound. Complaining to Grandpa that Eugene had beaten me, he replied, "Good"—and that was that. Never to complain again about what Eugene or Suzanne did to me.

Eugene came downstairs with an armful of flags and ropes as three German soldiers were ringing the doorbell. Suzanne was opening the door painted with a big red cross on the right side. I was right behind her— to see, as usual. The staircase to the upper floor came down in the same corridor, fortunately dark. Eugene rushed into the surgery room and hid the flags under the pad of the operating table.

This was 1944—after the landing. No more spic-and-span officers, organized, clean, well-fed German troops. After the opening of the Eastern Front in 1941, we had seen the deterioration of the German army. Most of their seasoned soldiers had been sent to the Russian Front, and those left were either young, very young, almost as young as I was, or old.

The three men at the door were young, dirty, disoriented. The one in the middle, supported by his comrades, could not have been more than 16 years old and was the one in obvious pain, crying. No blood,

Laure Reichek née Guyot

though. No visible wound. I do not know what Grandpa did to the soldier in surgery, but he said: "Poor kid— appendicitis. They understood that they must take him to a hospital. I don't know if he'll make it in time. I gave him a shot. What a waste!" When Eugene was changing the sheet on the pad, I saw the flag ropes and the corner of the Canadian flag—so difficult to paint that little cluster of three trees—sticking out.

In less than 24 hours, the whole town knew that Bigoudi had saved us—for the moment at least—from potential disaster. He had been the one to spread the news. So Bigoudi was honored and feasted the usual way. That day and for another week. A few more liters.

Laure Reichek née Guyot

Monsieur Gauthier

Chateaumeillant, Cher, France, 1936–1938

Monsieur Gauthier loved "his" titmice.

He had installed many birdfeeders in his beautiful garden. His days, since his retirement as a mail carrier, were devoted to the upkeep of his mini-paradise and its winged visitors. It would have been hard to tell whether he had trained his avian friends or whether they had trained him.

They flew toward him as he came out of his small house several times a day to assure himself that the platforms and feeders he had built throughout his garden were fully stocked with crushed seeds and small cakes of suet.

His enemies, sworn enemies, were the neighborhood feral cats that would come onto his property and lay in wait for a chance to catch one of "his birds." Mr. Gauthier was the self-appointed nurturer, defender, protector of the birds in "his" domain. A war was on, and Mr. Gauthier was determined to win it.

And he almost did.

First, he installed dangling bells in his fruit trees. Then, he bought a stuffed dog that could only be put out on nice sunny days.

Laure Reichek née Guyot

One day, Monsieur Gauthier bragged to my grandfather that he had finally, definitely solved his "cat problem." His solution was a 20-gauge. At dawn and at dusk, he would wait for the uninvited visitors and dispatch them quickly to the status of former visitors. Mr. Gauthier would then bury the dead animal at the foot of his trees, insisting that it made perfect fertilizer.

Monsieur Gauthier was beaten by a flea from the body of an "offender" and died of a plague-like ailment.

This was before the Second World War, before antibiotics had been introduced to Europe. Mr. Gauthier had been a single man and left no one to take care of "his birds."

I had observed that most people either liked cats or dogs; my grandfather did not like cats and definitely liked dogs, even loved them. I inherited his inclination and spent a lot of time in the company of dogs. There had never been a cat in my grandfather's house, but there were many dogs—retrievers, such as cocker spaniels, who were allowed in the house and with whom I was allowed to play as I wished. Grandpa and the cockers hunted small game, such as birds and rabbits.

The long-eared dogs, the Petits Bleu de Gascogne, the "little blues", were kept apart and were used for hunting big game, such as boar or bucks. These did not

Laure Reichek née *Guyot*

**Laure's Grandfather-Papa, Docteur Guyot,
with Aspro and Ultra (Petits Bleu de Gascogne)
and two hunting beagles**

belong to Grandpa but to an association of men who would hunt together.

They were kept in a separate building in the courtyard, and Monsieur Delebarre was in charge of their upkeep. He exercised them every day in the fields and forest on the edge of town. I was not allowed to go and play with them, but I often did. I could always tell when Grandpa was out visiting patients, since his car was not in the garage. That allowed me to sneak out to the doghouse, and Monsieur Delebarre let me.

Laure Reichek née *Guyot*

I found their ears irresistible and they seemed to enjoy my caresses.

And their voices! Oh, yes, I loved their bark, deep bassos, "aooh, aooh."

Since Grandpa and his hunting friends were all doctors or surgeons from other towns, all the dogs had been given medical terms as names, all six of them. I remember Aspro and Ultra (for ultraviolet) and X (for *radon X,* precursor to x-ray).

I like to think that they had a good life, fulfilled their destinies.

Laure Reichek née Guyot

The Twins
Chateaumeillant, Cher, France, 1938

Oh, yes, they had names. They were named Alain and Albert. But we called them the twins because they were impossible to distinguish.

When very young, their father hung himself shortly after the death of his wife from tuberculosis, so they had been brought up by their paternal uncle and his wife. Since their uncle and aunt were childless, it was natural that they had taken the role of parents.

This was before the war and the invention of antibiotics. Many persons suffered from tuberculosis there and in the countryside; the only treatment was a long and painful course of weekly injections of air—yes, air—around the infected areas in the lungs, since the bacillus is anaerobic. Success depended mainly on early detection. In the case of the twin's mother, her infection was very advanced, according to Grandpa, who had seen her shortly before her death.

Their uncle made harnesses and all things having to do with horses and wagons, as well as mattresses. (In those days, when a couple was married, they had a mattress made—a mattress that lasted a lifetime and often more.) His shop, with living quarters above, was directly across from the boys' school, so the twins had only to cross the street to attend classes. They were

Laure Reichek née Guyot

quiet, obedient, gentle boys and grew up learning their uncle's trade.

To the right of the shop was a vacant lot in which farmers would park their wagons on market days. Next to this empty space were the kilns, where limestone was blasted to become powder used in mortar for construction. Farmers also used the limestone powder to amend their land and to make paint for walls and for the trunks of fruit trees to protect against pests.

On the left side of the shop three houses: one belonging to a notary; one to the headmistress of the girls' school, the feared Mademoiselle Chatelain; and the last one to Monsieur Laporte, one of the three cobblers in town.

All the houses in town touched each other and shared walls with their neighbors. They were all the same design and size; only the fronts had sometimes been modified to include a large display window.

The houses all had the shop or store in front and the kitchen at the back, looking out on a long narrow garden. The well was usually in the garden, as was the outhouse. At night or in winter, people used chamber pots. Bedrooms were always upstairs.

When their guardians died, the twins became the sole owners of the shop and continued their trade in their predictable, quiet, simple way. They were excellent craftsmen, quiet men liked by everyone in town. They did

Laure Reichek née Guyot

not go to church on Sundays and did not frequent cafés, but they were often seen smoking a cigarette together in front of the shop during a break from stitching and gluing leather at their long workbench.

Having inherited a trumpet from their uncle, they both played in the municipal band that rehearsed once a month in the town hall. The band performed several times a year—on Bastille's day, Christmas and Easter theatrical events, and in processions of the various trade guilds.

Their lives were shattered on a Friday afternoon when the widow Pitault entered their shop to have her horse's reins repaired. Madame Pitault had just picked up her son after school to take him home to the farm she managed alone after the death of her husband from pneumonia. This is before antibiotics, and farmers did not go to see a doctor if they couldn't afford the time or, if required, the money.

Most diseases usually get better on their own anyway; doctors and dentists cost money, and you did not have the time to saddle a horse or hitch a wagon to go see a doctor or dentist who is going to send you to spend more money at the pharmacist when you should be doing an important task on the farm. That's what farmers thought and said in those days before mechanization, electricity, and water came to the isolated farms scattered around Berry.

Laure Reichek née *Guyot*

Since the 60s, most of those farms have been abandoned, many destroyed. Yes, it is sad. This part of France has a poor soil, cold winters, hot summers. Even big cities like Bourges have many empty houses with for-sale signs that have been there a long time. There are few industries in the area, so there are few jobs available for the grandchildren of the farmers. Oh, yes, there are still a few who manage to make a living in ecological projects, but there are few young people who can afford to buy ecologically grown farm products. Most of the buyers in those splendid farmers' markets are retired people, mostly old women, living on a guaranteed income.

So, to come back to the twins.

When the widow walked in their shop, followed by her six-year-old son, holding a torn rein, it was—well, we can only imagine. Madame Pitault was, in fact, a very handsome small woman, extremely neat in her attire, her dark hair tightly pulled back into a big chignon.

They must have felt thunderstruck, as in front of perfection, looking at an apparition. That was it. Instantly. Forever. Unfortunately, for both of them at the same time.

We know nothing of Madame Pitault's reaction, whether she was aware of the earthquake she had just created in those men's lives.

Laure Reichek née Guyot

We know nothing of the twins' suffering, their discussions, if they had any.

What we know is that a week later, a customer, finding the store open but empty, went upstairs and found the twins hanging side-by-side from the rafters of the attic where their father had hung himself 20 years earlier.

Hanging was the way used most often to end one's life. It was clean and cost nothing.

Very few farmers owned hand guns. Most owned a long gun, a prized possession used for hunting only. Cartridges were handmade, time consuming. Grandpa enlisted all of us to make cartridges every year before the hunting season.

When people in small towns died, families would hire persons, usually poor women, to go from door to door to inform everyone. There were few phones then, but news travelled faster than if phones were available because everyone shopped every day for bread and all the other necessities. Stores were not only places to buy meat, coffee, or nails, they were also part of a system of information. Each store had unique news, eagerly shared.

So by the end of the day, everyone knew the details of their deaths and, a few days later, everyone knew the time of the funeral. No one was surprised by their deaths

Laure Reichek née *Guyot*

or the method they had used. Everyone had been aware of their plight.

Since the twins had been respected for their hard labor, exemplary life style, good humor, and the quality of their work, not to mention the curious circumstances of their death, every able-bodied person in the town of 2,000 went to their funeral.

There had been no church service, since the twins did not attend services. Neither their father nor the uncle had attended services, so they did not, being as traditional as those who went to church regularly because their parents had.

This part of France was not known for its religiosity. People went to church for baptisms, weddings, and funerals. Daily and weekly services were attended mostly by a few old women. Few men ever went there and would have thought it unmanly, although their widows whould have a mass for them on their demises. Just in case.

Most young girls and boys living in town had attended cathechism and received communion, but those living in remote farms had not.

Their caskets were carried from the shop to the cemetery by a horse-drawn wagon and interred next to their mother and father. My grandmother and I were in the huge procession of townspeople that followed the hearse.

Laure Reichek née *Guyot*

The *cortege* was huge and noisy. I had been to funerals before, and I found it odd that people talked about everything except the defunct. But That day, everyone spoke of the beauty of their act, the romance of it, the inevitability of their dual suicides, about history revisiting history etc., but mostly about the shop and, since the twins had no heirs, who would replace them at their bench. Many also wondered whether they would be capable of hanging themselves, the mechanics of hanging oneself, the best way to ensure success.

Next to my grandmother and me in the long procession was a woman with a young boy about 8 or 10 years old, my age. Everyone within earshot heard the little boy ask his monther why Madame Demenois could not have had two husbands. For that question, the boy got a gentle cuff on the head, something he must have been used to because he continued: "Papa says the mayor has two women, so why can't a woman have two husbands?" In French, the word for woman and wife is the same.

His mother answered him, "I'll explain it to you later when we get home."

Being a girl, I already knew more than a boy my age about such things, but I kept my mouth shut while everyone around us giggled politely as if to say: "What children won't say next?"

Alain and Albert were 25 years old.

Laure Reichek née Guyot

The Pen

Chateaumeillant, Cher, France, 1937–1938

We all had, more or less, the same pen—a polished wooden shaft, a little longer than a pencil, fatter at the end where the metal nib was inserted, tapered at the other end.

In our desks, we had a box of nibs, fine ones for regular cursive and slightly bigger ones to write titles and for special effects. The ink wells were inserted in our desks and replenished every morning by the teacher. The pencils were used to do our prep work in special notebooks, called *brouillons*, in which we practiced before transferring our work into the regular notebooks from which we were graded.

We had two notebooks, one for writing, with horizontal and diagonal lines to guide us in writing straight with the proper inclines, and the other with unlined pages to do over our additions, subtractions and, later, multiplications. The higher grades had many notebooks, for geography, history, natural sciences, drawings and art.

Our pens, like our grey smocks hung on pegs on the far wall of the classroom opposite the teacher's desk, were pretty much all the same.

Laure Reichek née Guyot

Except...except Jeanine Gaillard's pen.

Jeanine lived on the same block on the main street, three doors up from our house, and sat at the desk next to mine. I say "three doors up" because the street rose in elevation before flattening on the plateau where the water pump was and the market was held every Friday.

Farmers came to market with their goods in horse-drawn wagons and had to pay a toll before entering the town. There, an employee of the town collected a fee at each end of the main road. Another fee was collected at the end of the day, based on the amount of merchandise sold during the day.

Like most French towns built at the end of the 18th century, the houses of unpainted stucco were aligned side by side on each side of the road, only one house deep, with a garden in the back. Only stores had a wooden façade and large glass widows with their displays of shoes, cloth or hardware, breads, meats. The farrier, wood and coal merchant had open yards where you could enter with your horse and wagon.

There were very few cars, no running water, no sewer systems. Electricity was installed later, after the war, but it did not extend to the outlying hamlets or isolated farms.

The traveling, itinerant merchants, who went from town to town on different market days, had small *camionettes* (small delivery vans) to carry their goods:

Laure Reichek née Guyot

working clothes, rubber boots, veterinary supplies, hardware, pots and pans.

The bazaar was a large tent of canvas, sheltering tables covered with stationary supplies, notebooks, pens, pencils of all colors, chalk, slates, drawing pads, rubber bands, small toys made in Japan, marbles, threads and needles, scissors, zippers and buttons. All objects cost less than one franc. It was called the "Bazaar à 20 Sous" (the Bazaar at 20 Cents).

All the school children would rush to the bazaar at the lunch break. Most of us did not have the few cents to buy anything, but we all went to look. I especially coveted the tiny colored paper flowers from Japan that would open up to reveal lotuses and chrysanthemums when you put them in a glass of water; they conjured up a world of mystery and exoticism.

Some of the pens displayed were prettier than the ones we used and were also a source of fascination. None we ever saw were as elegant, as fascinating and beautiful, as Jeanine's.

Her pen was made of white bone. The thin end up in the air was terminated by a carved small fan-like piece in which was inserted a small glass bead. When held closely to the eye, a landscape was revealed inside the bead. Jeanine had received the pen from an uncle who had gone to Vichy, then a renowned spa where people went to "cure" various ailments, especially of the liver,

Laure Reichek née *Guyot*

by drinking the water from ancient springs used by the Romans.

The landscape in the little marble showed a mountain with snow and a town at the bottom. To us, it was magic and beautiful.

Jeanine was not a pretty girl. She was the tallest girl in our class, very tall for her age. Her features were plain, her hair a nondescript chestnut brown, and her way of moving, her allure, was very ungainly: her feet were too big. She was not a very good pupil, could not sing, could not do most of the gymnastics. Under the roof-covered, open area where we did our physical exercises every day, was a straight rope, trapeze and rings, and parallel bars. Jeanine had never been able to lift herself off the ground—perhaps her large feet and heavy bottom prevented her from springing up.

We would have made fun, ridiculed someone else unable to do what everyone else could. But we did not embarrass Jeanine. Because she was the owner of that wonderful pen. She allowed each of us to hold it and peer through the marble, sometimes—sometimes not. She knew that her pen was her key, her passport to our games at recess when we played "house," or "school" in the empty coal bin in the yard, by drawing the outlines of rooms in the ground with a stick, complete with drawing tables, beds, stoves or teachers' and pupils' desks. All Jeanine had to do was to present herself and

say, "Can I play?" and she was "in." Because of the pen. We knew it and she knew it. No one need say, "Can I look at your pen later?" We knew value.

And the pen was of great value to us, like the skin of an orange or tangerine. Very few families could afford such fruits, a rare, tropical delicacy coming then from Africa or Spain. An orange was a Christmas present worth dreaming of. The lucky recipient of such a gift could barter the use of the skin for favors. It was loaned on an hourly basis, and the borrower could wrap it in her handkerchief to transfer the essence and carry it in her pocket as a treasure. Every day the piece of rind lost some of its value, as the skin became dry, odorless, and the magic evaporated. The fee became cheaper.

The pen, on the other hand, never lost anything. It was there for the whole class to see each time Jeanine opened her little wooden box with the sliding lid. We all had such a box in our *cartables,* in which we carried our notebooks and our homework to and from school. Some cartables were made of heavy canvas, some of leather, which we recognized as superior. The farm children had cloth bags, the merchants' daughters had leather bags.

Jeanine, of course, had a leather satchel. Her parent owned the *charcuterie,* located, like our house, on the main street. There was another charcuterie in town, but it was not on the main road with a fancy glass front, sparkling clean, with hyacinths in pots among the display

Laure Reichek née Guyot

of sausages, salamis, and patés, cornichons in glass jars, and even pickled mushrooms at holiday times.

Jeanine's father, Monsieur Gaillard, was a huge man, probably the tallest man in town. His workshop was in the basement of their house, where he chopped ground meat with a hand grinder and filled cleaned animal guts with meats for sausages and salamis. Hams hung from hooks in the ceilings. There was no refrigerator and no one had ever seen one, but there was a cold room filled with ice blocks, and the basement was itself very cold. Sometimes, in the summer, my grandmother would send me to get a few pieces of ice to be put into drinks.

Monsieur Gaillard, whom I called Papa, as I called many men in town, was a gentle man, soft spoken, generous with his time and, I think, exceptionally affectionate with me, since my grandfather was his doctor and neighbor. Madame Gaillard was a small dark-haired woman who rarely smiled—she kept the store upstairs.

Usually in the rest of her house, meticulously maintained, she would rush to the front as soon as the bell installed on the back of the front door rang. She served her customers with cold efficiency after donning an immaculate white apron hung between the living room, dining room, and the store. I never knew whether she was really "like that" or whether she played a role that had become a habit. No one in town would have

Laure Reichek née Guyot

called her a pleasant person, but her husband was esteemed as a splendid *charcutier* and a good, honest man.

Jeanine was their only daughter and knew that she would take her mother's place later. Obviously, she had inherited her father's physical appearance, down to the big feet, but she had the reserved behavior of her mother, a certain coldness with others. Perhaps her unusual height was responsible for that look of haughtiness, nose turned upward, away, naturally above the rest of us.

Still, living three doors up the street and being the only other girl in that bend of the road, she was my natural playmate. The games for girls were simple: we played house or school, our models. Only the boys played ball. Playing house was to delineate areas as kitchen and bedrooms and to mimic the roles of our parents—or in my case, grandparents—going in and out of the spaces, imagining doors, windows, walls.

The "father" would go out to work, come home, play with the children. The "mother" would cook on the imaginary stove when there was not a toy one, clean and dress the babies, sweep and dust the house, entertain neighbors with "tea sets" or cups and saucers borrowed from the real mother. Playing school meant taking turns being teacher or student, giving assignments and orders and fulfilling them.

Laure Reichek née Guyot

I had greater fondness for an older girl called Rosette who lived a little farther—maybe three hundred feet—but her playmates were already teenagers. Her father and my grandfather played bridge in the evening together, and he was a well-informed man who shared my grandfather's political leaning to the left. I sometimes went to play with her and her friends, but I was always assigned the role of baby or child because of my age.

With Jeanine, by necessity, I was either father or mother, and that gave me a better feeling, although I wished that I could be older and play the same roles with Rosette.

Rosette's parents owned the Emporium, a general store on the main square where you could buy furniture, baby buggies, dishes, notions, even bicycles. The store was the largest house in town, with an upper floor filled with furniture where it was a delight to play house.

Rosette was pretty, dark-haired and always the best-dressed girl in town. But she was older and she did not live almost next door. I could not come unannounced and say, "Can I play?" the way I could at Jeanine's house, knowing that she would be there and that I could go to the basement anytime to watch her father work.

Her grandmother made pâtés, lined up in the cold room in identical terra cotta tureens before being sent upstairs to the store to replenish the supply. They gave me my inspiration to play "store" when I was alone at

Laure Reichek née Guyot

home, putting identical pieces of cut paper in a row to represent the pâtés, and cut pieces of kindling became salamis and sausages. Hams were drawn on paper.

In my imaginary store in a corner of the kitchen, I would be both Madame Gaillard and her customers. As customer, I would enter the store, order something, ask how much it cost; then, changing position, I would give greetings, answer as Madame Gaillard, give prices and change by counting imaginary coins, small rocks, and a few buttons.

I really did not like Jeanine as much as I liked other girls, especially Rosette. Sometimes, I did not like her at all. But what could I do? She lived almost next door, and she owned that marvelous pen that she allowed me to hold, sometimes.

And that had to be enough.

The trouble began on a Tuesday morning, as we were filing out of the classroom toward the covered area where we did our daily gymnastics. From the rafters, hung the rings and straight ropes. Marie-Rose, who had been several rows behind me, managed to come beside me.

"Wait 'till you hear what happened," she said.

"What?"

"The pen has disappeared."

Laure Reichek née Guyot

"How?"

"Disappeared, you dope. Dis-a-ppeared. It's not there, and Jeanine has told Mme Perrin."

I was speechless. How could such an object disappear? It stuck out like a chandelier in a stable.

"What are we going to do?"

"Well, I don't know, but it better be found soon or we will all be under suspicion."

"Why?"

"What else?"

The enormity of the news was beginning to sink in.

"Who do you think could have stolen it?"

"Stolen? Oh my God!"

Jeanine's feet were on the ground as she was trying to lift her big body up to no avail. As usual, her bottom just weighed her down. She tried, her arms in the right position above her head clutching the rope with all her might, trying to lift the rest of her body, but there was nothing doing. Her legs could not push the earth away. There was just no spring in her. She had never been able to do it and never would. All she could do was squat.

Normally, we who could climb the rope would have rolled our eyes with a mixture of disdain and sympathy, but today we were all sympathy and Jeanine looked

around with the face of someone in the condolences line at a funeral. We all wanted to express our sympathy but dared not, afraid that it might imply complicity.

But we knew that everyone else in our class knew. Jeanine's mother, being an assiduous churchgoer, had told Father Morin, so it was no surprise when, next Sunday, his sermon focused on the commandments. When he got to the one about not coveting your neighbor's wife, he added: "And that goes for coveting anything. Do you hear me, children?" We of Mme Perrin's class knew what he was referring to. By now, we knew what coveting was.

According to the catechism class, when asked to describe coveting, the good father had explained that it was something before fornication and that it led directly to Hell. Outside of the church we had giggled ourselves silly. In a small town of less than 2,000 inhabitants, everyone knew who was fornicating with whom. And, for the ones younger than ourselves, we showed the superiority of our knowledge by using hand language description of the act, which we had seen the older boys make. You put the middle finger of your right hand next to the end of your right thumb. Then, having formed a hole, you inserted your left index finger into the circle and moved it back and forth. Most of the younger girls knew enough already to understand the gesture, but there were still some who did not understand. We left

Laure Reichek née Guyot

them with disdain, calling them too young to know the facts of life.

If the whole class knew of the theft, we assumed that the whole school knew. And if the whole school knew, then the whole town must know, since some girls had brothers in the boys' school.

We felt as if the whole town of 1,900 inhabitants was looking at us as coveters, thieves, and what not else. The pen had become as valuable as a work of art.

There were only 5 telephones in the village: the post office was number 1; the *gendarmerie* was number 2; the two doctors, Dr. Guyot and Dr. Touraton, were numbers 3 and 4, respectively; and the veterinarian, Mr. Lebrun, was number 5. To call, a farmer had to go by wagon or horseback to the nearest post office. Most people lived in isolated farmhouses or small hamlets, but wherever there was a café/restaurant/bread depot, there was a post office and a telephone. Of course, everyone could hear what you had to say, since one had to speak very loudly, sometimes scream, into the mouthpiece.

A few days later, the local gossip had it that the pen was made of gold with a precious stone embedded in it.

That is when my grandfather asked me into his office, sat me down across his desk where a patient normally sat, and asked, boring into my face with his x-ray eyes:

Laure Reichek née Guyot

"Did you take Jeanine's pen?"

There was no space for anything, any words other than yes or no. His eyes, as usual when he wanted, occupied every inch of my being.

"No," I said.

"Remember, when you want something that is not yours, you surrender your power, your money, and sometimes your life. You may go now."

Walking down the long, dark corridor to the living quarters, I pondered Grandpa's words. You did not take his teachings lightly. You paid attention. I think I got it, more or less. You paid attention to all Grandpas—their age endowed them automatically with knowledge of places and things, wisdom to analyze men's problems, experience to sort out others' feelings.

Grandmas, too, had their domain of knowledge, mostly in the world of women and children. Also, small animals. Of course, sometimes old folks lost their minds and their abilities. This was understood as the normal consequences of aging, like limping old dogs and lame horses, and did not deter in the least from our respect and sometimes awe toward our gray-haired neighbors.

That is the way it was 80 years ago in our small town in the center of France.

Laure Reichek née Guyot

P.S. The pen was found several months later in the dust of the coal bin in the corner of the yard where we used to play "house."

Jeanine married her father's apprentice and, when her parents died, she became the *charcutiére,* running the shop as her mother had, her husband working downstairs where her father had.

I visited her a few times, but we never talked about the "pen affair." There was still some guilt attached to it—from both sides. Still. When she died last year, her only son became the *charcutier.*

Laure Reichek née *Guyot*

The Infanticide

Chateaumeillant, Cher, France, 1937–1945

Monsieur Perronet had bought the café-restaurant around 1930 from the Renaud family, who had owned it since its beginning. It was situated on the main square, called La Grande Place, where the Friday outdoor market was held. There was another market, also on Fridays, less than a mile away on a place called the Champ de Foire, where cattle, oxen, cows, sheep, and pigs were sold. Only farmers in blue smocks and boots traded there. Few women or children went there.

The market on the Grande Place was where housewives went to buy butter, cheese, fruits and vegetables, and small animals like chickens or rabbits.

There were also many stands and vans with awnings selling sundries—ribbons, buttons, aprons. Also, a large tent with tables covered with school supplies, small toys, china and cutlery. On the Place was also a public pump, where many children on their lunch break would be sent to fetch water in large, vertical metal pitchers called *brocs,* since most houses did not have running water. Friday was the day of excitement for the children. So many people gathered in one place for a few hours. So many things to see. So much noise.

Laure Reichek née Guyot

The café had a few tables and chairs outside with a short awning of faded green canvas. Its outdoor space was demarcated by two rows of privet bushes in wooden tubs, separating it on one side from the hardware store and the other side from the fabric shop.

On market days, all chairs were occupied by men only, since it was not considered a proper place for women. Men drank red or white local wines, smoked, talked loudly, and sometimes played cards—things that women did not do. But it was exciting to watch. It was understood that farmers, accustomed to working outdoors, spoke very loudly to each other and to animals in order to be heard over great distances. Women, on the other hand, were supposed to talk softly at all times, and, if you raised your voice, you were accused of being a horse cart driver, a *charretier.*

The café also had a restaurant room used on special occasions, such as weddings or guild meetings. There were several guilds in the town, representing metal workers, wood workers or wine makers. Each guild had its own parade with decorated chariots, a fanfare, or local musicians, and the day would end with a banquet. Women and children helped in making the crêpe-paper flowers that adorned the chariots but did not share in the banquet. This was a man's affair with much eating, drinking, and loud language probably not suited for delicate ears. But the parade was fun.

Laure Reichek née *Guyot*

Monsieur Perronet did most of the cooking on feast days with hired help in the kitchen. Every other day, Vincent was his only helper. Vincent was an older man with a limp caused by an injury in the First World War. He lived on the outskirts of town, was married, and had three children. Always cheerful, with black trousers, white collarless shirt, a black satin vest, a long white apron, and a folded dish towel on his left arm (to wipe tables). He shuffled, not without grace, between tables carrying glasses on a tray held above his head with his right arm.

Manon was the young woman who cleaned and washed the tiled floor, washed dishes, and cleaned the apartment above, where Monsieur, Madame, and Mademoiselle Perronet lived. Manon had been in foster care since her birth but had recently reached her fourteenth birthday and had been released from the "Assistance" to work for wages. She had a room in the attic. The café was her whole world and she rarely left it. She was considered competent, clean, diligent, unassuming, and rarely noticed by anyone, since her work upstairs occupied most of her days.

She cleaned the café at the end of the day when most clients would have returned home or to their farms. A few men might stay in the evening to play a game of *belotte*, a card game, especially in summertime when the days were long. Few people would be outdoors when the days were long. In the evening people stayed

home, worked in their gardens, and children did their homework.

Madame Perronet would sometimes come down from her apartment to stand behind the cash register, sitting on a high stool. She was a very small person with grey hair and claimed to be always in bad health since the birth of her only daughter, now in boarding school, 15 years earlier. Her clothes were immaculate and of fashionable cut, the kind of clothes copied from fashion books by Madame Thevenin, a very good dressmaker, reputed to be the best. She wore no make-up and her hair was tied in a perfect chignon behind her head. She looked severe or pained.

Monsieur Perronet, on the other hand, was a large, vigorous, jovial man, always joking with his customers. He, like Vincent, wore black pants, white shirt, black vest, and a white apron.

All goods needed by the café—ice, wines, food stuff—were delivered by vans called *camionettes,* and the whole town could tell the days of the week by the vans in front of the café. One would say, "Oh! it must be Thursday; the ice van is here!" In a town of less than 2,000 inhabitants, everyone knew everyone, where everyone went, what came in, and what went out. We even knew every dog and every cat. They did not need collars to tell us to whom they belonged.

Laure Reichek née Guyot

Of course, everyone knew who had extra-marital affairs, where couples met (by the lake), or who had a mistress in another town. Farmers did not have affairs. How could they, stuck to their farms seven days a week? A few townspeople had vans. For example, Monsieur Dupuis, who owned the Emporium, the store that sold furniture, bicycles, baby buggies, had a delivery van. We knew that his van was seen parked for hours by the house of a widow in another village, and he was not delivering furniture. Well, good for him, everyone thought, his wife is a dried raisin.

Monsieur Perronet did not have a van. Madame Perronet stayed home upstairs. Manon stayed there, too. So, how could it happen that Manon was found in the *cabinet,* half dead in her bloodied skirts and petticoat by a customer needing to use the facility? The *cabinet* (the toilet) was at the end of the courtyard behind the café. A small wooden structure with a cement floor and a hole above the septic tank. No electric light and just a small hook inside the door. Barely four feet square. A stinking place in summertime.

The gendarme came and took Manon on a stretcher to the hospital and a few days later to an institution in a larger town where such women were to be re-habilitated. Some sort of special prison, we knew. Yet, no one had noticed that Manon was pregnant. No one ever noticed her, pushing her wet mop at the end of day or cleaning upstairs. Children from the "Assistance

Laure Reichek née Guyot

Publique" were sometimes more or less adopted by their foster parents, farmers who needed the money were paid by the government to take care of orphans or unwanted children. Sometimes they were exploited for their labor, but most of the time became one of their adoptive parents' family.

Every child from the "Assistance" had to go to school until the age of 14. All schoolchildren knew who was from the "Assistance". It meant that you would not continue your studies, since you would have to work, that you did not have a real father or mother to protect you unless you had formed a bond with your foster parents. And we all knew who considered their foster parents *parents* and who did not. Those who were not attached to their foster parents, who had been moved often from place to place, were regarded as lesser human beings, defective in some way. We never took into consideration the traumas or hardships they may have endured, since those pains were unknown to us. Therefore, it had to be their fault somehow, a defect of character, a lack of normal intelligence, a failure of will.

Since Manon had moved several times, from foster home to foster home, she was regarded as defective, mentally handicapped and, as such, erased, washed from the general consciousness. She was just there like the broom she pushed so assiduously in the café. How could anyone but a half-wit become pregnant and drop

Laure Reichek née Guyot

a baby in a septic tank? Did she even know she was pregnant? And by whom?

In a small rural town, everyone, including children above the age of eight, knew the facts of life. There were cows in the fields, rabbits in hutches in everybody's backyards, cats, dogs un-neutered everywhere.

That "girl" (that's what Manon was called in conversations) never went to the lake. Never went out. So?

"It takes two to tango, no?"

So, everybody put two and two together (or, rather, one and one) and came to the conclusion that only one man could have impregnated Manon.

My grandfather talked about the pain, the loneliness, the humiliation of the girl in that dark cabinet. How ignorance kills the soul and often the body. How terrible a sin it is for the society to treat women in such a cavalier, condescending manner. But his remarks were reserved for the family, around the table at dinnertime. Monsieur Leblanc, the veterinarian who came once a month to play bridge with my grandfather and shared his political views, understood and agreed. Both knew that Vincent could not have been the father, since he never was allowed upstairs, that he went home at the end of day on his rickety bicycle to his wife and children. That left only one man.

Laure Reichek née Guyot

He was never questioned by the authorities. The general consensus was to leave things alone. Why make a fuss? The thing was done, the girl was gone, and there were so many things to be attended to—the farms, the animals, the vineyards. Everything was forgotten, and we schoolchildren looked forward to the next Friday market.

Laure Reichek née Guyot

Monsieur George

Berry, Cher, France, 1957

He was known as Monsieur George, although everyone knew that he was the descendant of old nobility, albeit of a minor rank. Monsieur George, as he wanted to be called, was, by all opinion, a very handsome man, slightly above average height, built like an athlete, with carrot-red hair.

When he was recalled from medical school in his third year after his father had become ill and unable to take care of the estate, he found his father had hired a housekeeper, Simone. Monsieur George, aided by Simone, managed the estate well and gained the respect, even admiration, of the farmers in the region. He worked hard, and the fields and forest were in good order. He was not "stuck up" and was friendly and generous.

Simone was always cleaning, cooking, taking care of chickens and rabbits and the dogs that she loved. The vegetable garden and orchard were immaculate. Neighbors knew that she was always available to lend a hand at harvest time or to help in preparations for ceremonies of any kind. She was also a very good dancer and was sought after as a dance partner at wedding feasts and festivals.

After the death of his parents, Monsieur George became the master of the manor and Simone became

Laure Reichek née Guyot

the de-facto mistress, although she continued to behave as the housekeeper she had been destined to be.

The manor was a large two-story structure, unlike most farmhouses of the region that had only a ground floor and, often, only one large room. The building was neither pretentious nor particularly handsome. The house was hidden from the main road by a small forest of oaks and chestnuts.

manor house, Cher, Berry, France

I remember going there once with my grandfather, who had been the doctor of the old "count"; I had heard my grandfather say that the "countess" had died many years earlier of breast cancer, necessitating the hiring of Simone. The "count" lived at least 15 years after his

Laure Reichek née Guyot

wife's death. My grandfather had been very impressed by the place and thoroughly entertained by Simone, who had allowed me to play with a new litter of cocker spaniels kept in the kitchen. The year must have been 1937 or 1938.

Where Simone came from I did not know or do not remember; nor can I say how old she was, since all adults looked old to me, but she must have been in her early 20s. She was a most efficient and agreeable person. Her straight, thick, very dark hair was braided, tied behind her head, and covered with a triangular scarf. On her feet, she wore *sabots* (wooden clogs). She always wore two aprons, the working one on top of the clean one, and would always remove the working one when there were visitors in the house.

Her most striking feature was her extremely dark and large eyes, like those of my grandmother, a reminder of the passage of Moors and Saracens through that part of the world that had not changed much since the 8th century.

Because of her unusual good looks, people of the neighborhood assumed (behind her back) that she was the illegitimate child of some defunct nobleman, friend, or acquaintance of Monsieur George's father. Since there were many young men and women adopted by farmers from the Assistance Publique (the national orphan association), this was not considered a handicap. Many,

Laure Reichek née *Guyot*

usually poor sharecroppers or farmers, were paid by the government to adopt orphaned children. Many of these children were treated as their own children by their adoptive parents and grew up, married, had children of their own, and remained in the same area.

After visiting the "count" with my grandfather, I forgot about the place, the people there, the people of that country. Other concerns took all my time. I moved to another country, another continent, a new family demanded my attention.

The next time I found myself back in the places of my early childhood was 1957, 20 years later, after a war had ravaged Europe; many places had disappeared, while others were in the process of reconstruction on a different model.

I was in a bus going southeast from Châteroux to visit my grandmother, who was still alive, living alone on the edge of a small town, Chateaumeillant. Next to me on the bus was an old man in a dark green corduroy suit, obviously his best clothes. I imagine he was going to a large town, perhaps to see a medical specialist or visit some relative for important business. My eyes were glued to the passing landscape viewed through my window when I suddenly recognized the place. The small road was there, on the left, but the trees were gone and there was no building in the empty space. I was shocked and, before the sight disappeared, I asked

my neighbor if there had not been a manor there. *"Oh, oui, Madame,"* he said, with a Berrichon patois, *"y zont tout razé"* (they have razed everything).

The smell of cows and hay coming from the man's clothes made it easy to switch language, and we continued the conversation until we arrived at my destination, stopping often along the way in tiny hamlets to let out schoolchildren going home at the end of the day and farmers on the way back from errands in Châteroux.

I learned then about the events that led to the destruction of a place in which a pleasant memory had been buried for 20 years of my life. The story is not pleasant, as is true of so many stories of war, when men are encouraged to manifest the cruelty of which they are capable in the name of patriotism or exceptionalism.

I introduced myself to my traveling companion, who also gave me his name. He, of course, had also known my grandfather, as had his own doctor in the town of Châteroux, where our trip had started.

I told Monsieur L my grandfather had hunted grouse with Monsieur George many years ago and asked whether there were still any game on the property.

"Oh, ma pov dam, y'a pu d'bouchures pour ces pov ptites creatures pour fare leurs nids. Y z'ont tout enlevé y'a pu d'gibier. Y'a pu rien. C'est mort." (Oh, my dear lady, there are no longer any hedgerows for the little creatures

Laure Reichek née Guyot

to make their nests. They removed everything. There is no longer anything. It is dead.)

Monsieur L then told me the following story.

During the occupation, small resistance groups were formed in the southern part of our province, Berry, and in the Central Mountains. Monsieur George's house became a center of resistance in 1943 and continued to organize "partisans" until 1944, when he was denounced by another farmer who had been and remained a faithful follower of Maréchal Pétain. The manor was raided by the Milice (French police collaborating with the Germans).

When the truck arrived, Monsieur George was in the stable. He was led out to a car. Simone who had witnessed the arrest, ran toward the uniformed men and told them: "Whatever happens to him should happen to me." She was also taken into the car. They were driven to the side of the main road, executed, and left there for all to see. Their bodies were removed by friends during the night, and no one knows where they were buried.

In the loft of the stable, playing in the hay with Monsieur George's permission, was the son of Monsieur L. Monsieur George, who heard the truck coming, told the child: "Do not move, do not make a sound," thereby saving the life of Monsieur L's son.

This was in May 1944, one month before the Allies landed in Normandy. The property has been sold many

Laure Reichek née Guyot

times since and is now owned by Belgians, who come only once a year in the summertime and live in the modernized old stable and haybarn.

Monsieur L said that he had not been there since that day, did not care to, and that I would understand why.

Laure Reichek née Guyot

Conversation

Petaluma, CA, USA , 2008–2016

• Why do you need to believe that some men are good?

• Because, I suppose, I don't want to believe that the whole enterprise is a mistake.

• Is it?

• Mostly, I think, yes. Men are not finished. They are still evolving. He has to perfect himself constantly. Evolution, you know.

• Do you know some good men?

• Good in parts—yes—some better than others.

• Good. Better—naturally?

• Naturally? No. I think all possibilities are there at the start. It depends which ones are encouraged, nurtured, valued. On the time, the place, the circumstances, the mother.

• Why do you add the mother?

• Because I think she transmits the good, the shameful, and the bad of any culture. She is made to forget her dependent behavior, her collaboration with trinkets, turned into a shopping addict.

• And the father?

Laure Reichek née Guyot

- Oh, the poor bugger, he is not to be trusted. His convictions; his principles are determined by his vanity and his financial interests. Wants to appear bigger, richer, smarter than he is.

- Aren't there places where it does not apply?

- I don't think so. But it takes different forms.

- I'm afraid so.

- Then how can change happen?

- Violently, when we can no longer breath, when our waters will be undrinkable and decent food, housing unaffordable.

- Why does it have to be violent?

- Because people always hope that change will happen by itself or that others will make it happen. When nothing changes in their lives' time and they see no hope in sight—then, only then, they rebel.

- They have to be deeply affected and have nothing to lose. Is that what you're saying?

- Yes, change is always violent—birth of anything, new lands from volcanic eruptions, human and animal birth, cracking glaciers—the whole natural order of cat eat mouse.

- Whoa! That's not a very pretty picture!

Laure Reichek née Guyot

- It can be beautiful, too, if that is your priority. There is enough natural beauty for man to emulate. Artists know about that. There are beautiful thoughts articulated in poetry, music, painting, dancing, architecture, even those that depict pain, ugliness and despair.

- Why do you call it beautiful if it depicts ugliness?

- Because it teaches us about ourselves and what we are capable of doing, thinking, feeling.

- How can that be violent?

- It is violent in the sense that it displaces a preconceived view, a deeply ingrained prejudice or accepted assumption.

Exact Title and Structure Unclear

Petaluma , CA, USA 2008–2016

"An Augean stable of metallic filth"
—D. H. Laurence

King Augeas had 3000 oxen kept in stables uncleaned for 30 years. Imagine!

On my first visit here 50 years ago, I had already noticed how noisy and dirty it was.

But now! Even the North and South Poles, where no one lives, are littered with garbage, mostly plastics, in and out of the water.

Every one uses a vehicle, even to go a few blocks. Gasoline driven machines! (in 2010!) The air is saturated with CO_2. They still use coal to fire furnaces, too! They have to purify their water. Their seas, rivers, lakes are fouled by leaching pesticides, oil, and chemicals. What are their scientists thinking? How can they keep on using the same methods of producing food and goods?

Their cities! So big that at times the traffic does not move. Their buildings, even their dwellings, are huge. Families do not share space. Everyone has a separate room and a separate bath.

Laure Reichek née Guyot

REPORT ON THE LIFESTYLE OF
THE MIDDLE CLASS IN MIDDLE WORLD

The first thing to strike the visitor is the size of things. Their houses are huge. They do not share space if they can avoid it. Each bedroom has a bath. There is even one in the hallway for visitors and a closet to hang coats.

There is a garage for several cars. Each one living in the house has a car, sometimes two, and a truck. They have every imaginable tool for gardening and carpentry, just in case you need it. There are bicycles, skis, sometimes even a boat. The garage is that big.

The kitchen has all the gadgets a professional cook needs; a granite center counter to prepare food for a battalion where they only fix a breakfast of cereal and milk.

They are rarely home during the day, for both adults work hard in some store or office. Their garden is magnificent—a copy of one advertised in the glossy "Home" magazines. A maid comes to clean house twice a week, and a gardener maintains the showcase grounds. Most of the material used in the building of the house, from the floor tiles in the kitchen and baths to the plumbing fixtures, are imported from other countries. The architecture replicates the elements of Italian villas,

Laure Reichek née Guyot

English manors or French country houses. Most of the cars are also imports.

They produce an enormous amount of garbage, debris and discards. Their dumping grounds have as much acreage as small towns. Many of the objects thrown away—furniture, toys, tools, house fixtures—are in good working order.

Their lands and water are polluted by toxic materials leaching into the soil. Plastics float everywhere. Their agricultural practices destroy the land they exploit. Very few wild plants and animals survive the encroachment of their habitats by constant housing development accompanied by its polluting consequences.

The two children (ideally, two—a boy and a girl) go to high school in their own cars. The parents leave for work at the same time or earlier, each independent of the other. The children choose their clothes, their foods, their entertainment. They rarely eat together except on organized trips or at a once-a-year clan gathering. Most of the time, they keep in touch with each other via cell phones. They keep in touch with their friends via email or texting. They call it "doing your own thing."

Everyone constantly talks on their cell phones: from their cars, their houses, inside stores. They seem lost when not holding the gadget to their ears. They need to tell someone where they are, what they are doing, seeing, hearing, feeling, perhaps. Even their cars tell

Laure Reichek née Guyot

them where they are, as if they could not read a map or ask directions. They feel lost without it, as if others were not to be trusted, themselves included.

Without all this metallic and electronic technology, they do not know who and/or what they are. Without it, they are bored and feel inadequate, incomplete, humiliated.

Unfortunately, their acquisitions are obsolete or out of style the moment they buy them, so the desires for the latest thing called "better" is never fulfilled.

In their bathroom, the medicine cabinet looks like a mini-pharmacy. There are drugs for sleeping, for staying awake, for pains of all kinds, for stress management. They have many diseases of the body and the mind, hence their great consumption of pharmaceutical products.

Cosmetics abound, although they often go to a hair salon, sometimes once a week. They visit masseuses and chiropractors often. Although they own one or more exercise machines, they regularly go to "health clubs," where their movements are organized and supervised. They do not seem to be able to make any of the objects they use. Everything is imported from other parts of the planet, where some of them are kept poor in order to be forced to work in horrible, noisy, smelly, toxic places to produce what the MIDDLEWORLDERS need.

Laure Reichek née *Guyot*

The women seem to enjoy holding and playing with their offspring, but once these become teenagers, the parents despise them. The children, in turn, show no respect for their elders. When they reach sexual maturity, the children are given vehicles and sent to wars. There are always wars—one country invading another to control whatever mineral resources the invaders need. They repeat the experiences of the Greek and Romans, only the killing is faster and more efficient. Obsolete military hardware (planes, tanks, etc.) occupy miles of ancient grasslands. Functioning military camps and installations use up many thousands of acres more. Wars appear to be their accepted form of birth control.

Raising children is very expensive in MiddleWorld. To keep pace with the advertised view of success, parents must buy new clothes, new toys, new gadgets for their children, even if the ones they already have are still usable. Education costs a lot, and parents resent this investment if it does not bring the desired results, hence the disappointment and distance created between parents and offspring.

Very few Nacirema grow their own food. Everything is flown or trucked in, sometimes from very far places where other poorer people work on large plantations or industrial farms. They do not appear to know what food is good for them, for about one-third of them look visibly blown up, unhealthy. They also drink tremendous amounts of alcohol, not just on feast days.

Laure Reichek née Guyot

Their cities are noisy (mostly from their vehicles) and their air has a nasty odor. They release great amounts of carbon dioxide into the air from burning fossil fuels, which they then breathe. Their scientists may not have developed other energy sources yet.

They cannot stand silence. Their air is constantly filled with noises, metallic and electronic noises, many of them must damage their ears.

They cannot stand open spaces. Their parks, lakes, mountains and sea shores are crisscrossed by huge vehicles, boats, ski mobiles, snow mobiles, planes. The most remote of their deserts are invaded by SUV, motorcycles and airplanes. The Nacirema hate to walk except as an exercise.

What do they think they're doing to themselves and to the planet? Or do they?

Laure Reichek née Guyot

Casino

Petaluma, CA, USA, 2008–2016

Joe, my neighbor, told me about it: "Just get on your horse and go to look at the freeway from the hill, next Friday at 5 p.m." I did. Could not believe my eyes. Going north, bumper to bumper, not moving. Came back one hour later, and the car I'd mark as a reference had just moved half a mile. What the heck? Next day, I went by Joe's place about mid-morning thinking he'll have done his chores and maybe a cup of fresh coffee would accompany the chat. Right I was. We sat down in his cool kitchen, cool because there are trees all around his house, because it's painted white and sparsely furnished.

He is the one that started.

"Did you see it?", he said.

"Sure did, but where were they all going?", I asked back.

"There's a new casino right up the road a bit," he informed me.

"Son of a gun! Another one of those?"

"Yep."

"What do people see in them, I wonder?"

"More people, that's what they see."

Laure Reichek née *Guyot*

"What would they want to do that for, see more people?"

"Because they're lonely, I guess."

"Lonely? Don't they work?"

"Oh yeah, they work, they see people but they're still lonely."

"I sure don't get it. How do you get lonely when there's so much to do?"

"Maybe it's because they don't like what they do, or they don't care because it means nothing to them."

"How can you not like what you do and do it?"

"That's what most people do, Pete. They work to make money to buy things, but they don't like what they do. It has no meaning for them. Sometimes they just hate it but keep doing it to pay their mortgage or their rent, put food on the table, and send the kids to college. They can't stop once started—they have to keep going till they drop."

"But what's the casino got to do with that?"

"That's the escape, Pete. Escape in an artificial world where you see people like you, trying hard to see if God would smile on them, just for once."

"Oh, my God."

"You said it. You and I are alone but never lonely, but what we do is our lives. Taking care of the land and the animals. We're needed, and we do our job with all we've got. We sleep well because we are content to do what we do. No need for casinos for us. A new calf or a good rain has more meaning than their slot machines. A good neighbor like you means a lot, and you're good because you do, well, what you do. We have good times together—picnics, fishing, hunting, just sitting talking. Like now."

"Well, I guess we may be the last to feel that way."

"Yep."

Laure Reichek née Guyot

On the Threshold of Time

Petaluma, CA, USA, 2008–2016

There she sat, in a shaded alley in the Germaine Labordé park on Rue de Babylone, not because it was the neighborhood where she lived more than 50 years ago (the park did not exist then), not because she felt any nostalgia for the specific area (or did she?), but because it was a cool place to relax, contemplate, reflect, think about what she was doing there. Her trip had been planned with a friend from California where she had lived for the last 70 years, but her friend had a medical emergency a few days before their departure date. Now she was alone and feeling lonely. She had gone to the park before with her husband when he was alive and well.

The park was extremely attractive. Behind high walls that had once been part of a convent, then a women's prison, it was now dedicated to teaching children about edible plants and fruit trees. It had a large grassy area where workers on lunch break, students, nannies pushing babies, young children, could lounge on the grass while looking at impeccably maintained vegetable beds, bushes and trees. Gardeners were weeding, pruning, patiently explaining their work. It was an oasis in the middle of a busy city. Time there was measured by the needs of the plants.

Laure Reichek née Guyot

The temperature being about the same as that of the body, one's boundaries seemed to disappear, one's skin no longer existed, extended into the atmosphere itself. One became one with the space. Children running after balls, screaming in delight, the birds—pigeons, mostly—did not disturb the atmosphere. Every being felt right in the right place, a natural extension of the space.

She had stopped for lunch at the "Pied de Fouet", the old 19th-century bistro that had been a stagecoach stop at the beginning of the 19th century, a restaurant that still had the napkin case for the *habitués,* most of them government employees in the various ministries, embassies, consulates in the neighborhood who knew each other and came every day for lunch. The restaurant was small, with a small bar and one server. If you came at 12:20, you had to wait on the sidewalk with a glass of wine until a seat could be had, and you knew that the patrons had to go back to work at 1:00. The food was homestyle, generous and inexpensive. Nothing had changed there. The *toilette* was still outside in a small yard.

So, there she was, looking at the children, the few old people taking a rest after shopping or simply resting there as she was, an old woman herself, resting on a bench after lunch, looking at the people of all ages, shapes and colors in the park, listening to the sounds of children playing, conversations of nannies in Spanish,

Laure Reichek née Guyot

Portuguese, and African languages she did not know, the French students she barely understood, feeling the soft air that dissolved her.

Of course, memories intruded. The last time she was here after her husband's death, she found the apartment where they lived in Rue Vaneau in the late 1940s, an old *hôtel particulier,* had been renovated into a high-rent, high-security building that she could not enter. Like most buildings today, you needed to punch a code to open the front door. No more concierges.

On her previous visit to Paris, only five years earlier, she had been able to come into the courtyard and look at her old apartment, a converted stable on the ground floor, and had been able to see that the building was slated for remodeling. The flagstones in the courtyard were uneven, some broken, and the lawn had been neglected on purpose before the renovations were to take place.

A very old woman, led by an attendant, sat on the bench next to her. The woman was almost bent in two, a large hump on her back. She wore a skirt and jacket, dark blue, of a pre-war cut; one could not see the blouse, since her eyes faced the ground. When we say pre-war, we mean that for persons her age, history is divided into three parts: Pre-War, During the War, and After the War. Refer to any of those and people old enough know exactly what you mean. The atmosphere of that period,

Laure Reichek née Guyot

the images, sounds, smells are immediately conjured up. Who remembers when it took two days to go from Paris to Marseille? The sounds of sirens? The rationing tickets, the long lines to get a piece of bread, the dread of air raids, the smell of the shelters, of fear, the value of a bar of soap, the sound of bombs whistling down, the uniforms? Why, for us, During the War comes first in memory, comes before Before the War? The old lady knew.

Her attendant, bending close to her ear, said in a very loud voice, "I'll see if I can get you some", then apologized to the other woman on the bench, "She is very deaf." She got up and went to a row of raspberries across the alley to look for fruit, found a few and brought them back to her charge in the palm of her hand.

A dialogue followed between the attendant and the foreign woman—foreign now, although born here.

"How old is this lady?"

"She is 103, she says she wants to die but she can't."

"Has she no relatives here?"

"No, she is alone in the world now. They all died During the War. They were Jewish. She escaped because she was in the south, giving a concert. She was a great pianist in her day. Well known."

"Does she talk about it?"

Laure Reichek née Guyot

"No, she only says that she wants to die."

"Does she live in her apartment?"

"Yes. The State sees to that."

"Does she have a piano still?"

"Oh, yes, and although she has arthritis all over, as you can see, she still plays sometimes."

"Do you come here often?"

"Every day, if it is not raining. It gives her pleasure to see the children. Her eyes are still quite good. But she cannot hear them much except when they scream with joy. She likes that."

"Excuse me, but how can she play the piano if she cannot hear?"

"I asked her once, and she said you do not need to hear with your ears, that once you know something or someone, you hear them with your heart."

The visitor got up, said good-bye to the old pianist and her attendant, and realized, as she was walking out of the park, that she was hearing sounds that were not there. The sounds of a woman pianist playing a Beethoven sonata. "How appropriate and beautiful," she thought.

Laure Reichek née *Guyot*

Michel

Petaluma, CA, USA, October 2019

Laure (left) and Michel, 1939, the farm of Michel's parents

You died yesterday. I was not surprised. When we last spoke, about a month ago, I knew how deeply unhappy you were. More than unhappy. There are no words to express the depth of your pain, not just the physical pains you had endured for more than 40 years, after the fall that left your skeleton shattered—no, not that kind of pain, the kind that destroys not the person but the personality, the kind of pain that is the result of deep humiliation at the hands of someone one holds

Laure Reichek née Guyot

dear, the insult, assault to the core, the motor that keeps one running.

I knew you had lost the will to be, and I understood it. You had invested all of you in the construction and maintenance of Michel Meaulnes, the person you may have always wanted to be. A slow fabrication accelerated after your wife's death, taking all your time and energy, your waking hours in front of a screen, searching and researching, your sleeping hours in fantastic dreams, in Alain Fournier's world at the end of WWI located in the same area and where your grandparents lived, the identification complete once you moved to a street named after the famous author.

When I last saw you, you were spending your time in front of your computer, looking at photographs of your ancestors' farm and the manor house of the neighborhood. The last original inhabitants of that larger-than-most house had left only one descendant. You were in long-distance communication with her, you had fallen in love with her, completely, sight unseen. You had known her once as a girl of five; she had sent you a photograph showing the back of her head, and you had fallen in love with a long braid of what looked like blond hair, while she had seen a frontal photograph of you, sitting at a table.

You were in daily contact, sometimes several times a day. You were floating in a stratospheric amorous cloud,

Laure Reichek née Guyot

way above your walker and wheelchair, way above the diapers you were now obliged to wear.

I wish you had died then, a year ago, before the lady's visit, your humiliation and destruction.

After my visit, the lady of your dreams came, at your insistence and expense. It was a disaster—your words, as you spoke them to me the Monday after her departure, itself a snafu, since she got on the wrong train for her connection to the airport.

We spoke via long-distance phone calls every Monday morning, and I am glad I was there, as your oldest childhood friend, to receive your dreams, pains, stories. But, dear Michel, I wish you had died sooner.

Why could you not have contained your dream? Why did you need to concretize, materialize your desire, give substance to your thoughts? A sudden rush of youthful, hormonal needs? It had happened to you a year earlier when you had fallen in love with another patient while in the hospital. Remember? It had been stopped by the woman's family. You had been hurt but not badly enough; you had not yet learned.

So, what was it about this time? Needing to love and be loved is universal and you knew that. Possession, control of another? I don't think so, not in your case, not with your politics. So, what's left? Just being alive with oneself, a person one can respect, maybe admire a little. That means to be alive, really alive, till the end,

Laure Reichek née *Guyot*

the visibly approaching end. Did being alive mean to be in love, to be vibrant, vibrating with all the senses even if it ends in catastrophe?

Damn it, Michel, although I had wished for a while that you had died sooner, before the lady of your dreams came to demolish them and leave you empty, I woke up this morning thinking that I may have been wrong to agree with your other friends, that this had been the case.

I woke up with a question: What if we were all wrong and you had been right to invest yourself in what you knew to be your last chance to engage your self without reservation, expectation of success or reward of any kind? What if this had been a conscious decision? To be all of oneself in a last opportunity to feel totally human?

I do not know, and none of your friends will ever know. But the question raised this morning, after a forgotten dream, changes my view of your death.

If this new thought has any value, then I can only say, "Bravo, Michel."

You died well.

Laure Reichek née Guyot

Bombay There & Here

Bombay, India, Summer, 1963 and
Petaluma, CA, USA, April 2020

It was in the year 1963 that we—my husband, our two boys, and I—landed in then-called Bombay, late at night.

We had flown through a typhoon on the way from Hong Kong, where all, excepting only our children, had been on their knees, in the aisles, with their heads in brown paper bags.

The captain of that Pan Am had introduced himself as Buckshot Wayne in an old amused voice, followed by the announcement: "Folks, you better buckle up, it's going to be a rough ride."

I am sure none of the passengers had any idea of how rough it would be. Very rough, it was.

The next leg of our trip, north of Bombay, was to Ahmedabad. Instead of staying at the airport, waiting for our connection, we decided to go to a hotel and rest a few hours.

We were the only persons in the shuttle minibus, going through Bombay in the middle of the night. It was raining heavily; the monsoon had arrived. The streets were deserted, and the headlights of the van were

Laure Reichek née Guyot

throwing an eerie glow on the greyness through which we were going.

One of our sons, I don't remember which, asked, "What's that?"

"What's what?" I said.

"Those things on the sidewalk, there!"

I looked through the rain-streaked windows and saw long, white bundles, lying side by side in the rain. I did not know, could not recognize, what I was looking at, having never seen such things before.

My husband looked, as well, and, after a while, told us what those shapes were.

"Those are dead bodies, wrapped in cloth, waiting to be picked up for cremation."

This was our introduction to India, 1963, in a cholera epidemic.

It is now 2020. People move from one continent to the other in a few hours. Goods crisscross the skies and oceans constantly. Information and capital travel through space at vertiginous speeds.

This morning, I went shopping at an early hour in the comfort of my own automobile in the small town in Northern California where I live. Streets were almost deserted and non-essential shops closed. The Covid-19

Laure Reichek née Guyot

virus had, overnight, changed the landscape, visible and invisible.

Unhoused persons with various degrees of disabilities had been visible in our town for a long time, the existing homeless shelter being unable to answer to the needs of all unhoused people in our area. Most of them were wandering the streets around the shelter, where they could spend the night and receive food and counselling, if wanted.

Now, new regulations prevent you from wandering freely without masks, collecting trash that could be exchanged for money at the only recycling center, now closed.

What is the houseless population to do?

I counted 12 human body forms sleeping in doorways of closed shops.

Going around to the back of the homeless shelter, I counted 40 human beings leaning against the brick wall of a large store, facing the rising sun.

Flashback to Bombay, 1963.

Laure Reichek née Guyot

Of Eggs & Cheese
Baja California Sur, 1986 and
Petaluma, CA, USA, July 2020

Two miles down the road is a chicken farm. The birds roam freely in several large enclosures and are provided with moveable shelters on wheels, some looking like ancient gypsy caravans, others of unique, interesting designs. When the ground around the chicken houses is saturated with their droppings, the owner simply tows the caravans to another place with a tractor.

Eggs are sold in the driveway, stored in a cooler. Buyers help themselves, dropping the money in a closed box attached to the closed gate.

I have always admired the way the chickens are raised and treated and the way the farm is kept, but I cannot afford to pay the price, which is about twice as much as the most expensive eggs at the store where I do most of my shopping.

Today I stopped in the driveway to admire a newly installed huge chicken shelter. It was about a 50-foot-long structure with open canvas walls rolled up onto the roof to offer shade in the hot sun and air circulation the hard-walled caravans do not have.

Laure Reichek née *Guyot*

A notice on the gate announced that the price of eggs had been raised to $10 a dozen to offset the lack of customers and the increase in theft.

My first thought was: What are they going to do with all the eggs they cannot sell? Would it not be better to lower the price and attract more customers?

And that reminded me of another experience at a farm in another country, more than a thousand miles away. The year was 1986. My husband and I were in the southernmost tip of Baja California on the Sea of Cortez side where a friend had recommended an inexpensive, simple group of bungalows on a small bay called Cabo Pulmo.

We rented a car in San José del Cabo, a Volkswagen Bug with its roof sawed off and drove north, hugging the coast on what had not yet been developed as a road and must have been a riverbed in an ancient period of the planet. The road was very rough with many large stones to be avoided and others moved, but it was beautiful. The only other vehicle we encountered was a Volkswagen bus full of surfers. Their license plate said they were from Utah, and I could not help wondering where people from Utah learned to surf or how many hours they had to drive to get to an ocean.

We stopped at a place with bungalows but quickly learned that this was a deluxe resort and not the place we were looking for.

Laure Reichek née *Guyot*

We finally arrived at our destination, a small bay with a dozen small wooden bungalows, a restaurant, and several hangars where surfboards, canoes, and kayaks were kept for the use of guests. Children and a few dogs were running happily in the sand.

During the day, after a swim in the perfect waters or a kayak run, we would often return to San José del Cabo or go to the small towns north of the colony to explore.

One afternoon, in a café in San José Del Cabo, we met an American who spent half the year there and was familiar with most of the inhabitants in this part of Baja. After telling him where we were staying, he recommended we go visit a typical farm in the vicinity of Cabo Pulmo and taste their cheese. He gave us verbal directions and drew a map on a paper napkin. We went there the next day.

The place itself was rather barren and not extraordinary, but the Dominguez family was extraordinary—all rather tall and wide-shouldered, with the natural grace of caballeros. Señor Dominguez, and his wife had two sons and two daughters. Their house was a single long building with only one door and two windows on one side. Their clay oven was outside, as well as a large table and chairs covered by a palm-frond awning. The well was also conveniently located next to the oven.

Laure Reichek née Guyot

At the back of the house was a small stable for two horses and a shed where the daughters made cheese from the milk of four cows and four goats, who grazed on the brownish shrubs and chapparal.

We were offered cool lemonade, brought up from the bottom of the well in a pail, before being shown around the house. The main room was partitioned into bedrooms by hanging cloth. The young men slept on each side of the door, their sisters shared one wall, and the parents shared the longest portion of the opposite wall. Chests of drawers were arranged to make a low wall and an alley in the center of the space, at the end of which were closets.

The space immediately felt good, restful, uncomplicated, and yet very well designed. It was quite dark and cool.

We sat outside, talking with the help of Juanita, who was an avid reader of English and American writers. She had spent several years in school in San José del Cabo and loved English. Like most children from isolated farms all over the world, she stayed in town five nights a week with relatives and was brought home by her father when he came to deliver his wife's homemade cheeses.

We visited the small shed where the cheese was made. Like the rest of the place, it was immaculately clean and simple—shelves, wooden tubs, wooden

Laure Reichek née Guyot

ladles, no electricity, no machines. We were given some cheese to taste; it was simple, honest, yet flavorful.

We offered to buy some and asked, "How much do I owe you?", and Señor Dominguez said, "2 pesos." We were stunned and said, "But that is not enough for such good cheese!" Señor Dominguez replied, "But if I asked for more, the poor people could not buy it."

We looked at each other and at this family, and I hope that our eyes conveyed the admiration and love we felt for these people. All my husband said was, "That is very admirable of you." That is what happened, and I obviously never forgot it.

I stayed in touch with Juanita for about five years after our visit, and one day she did not answer. I hope she married as good a person as her father and mother and she is somewhere raising children who know their grandfather and grandmother.

Laure Reichek née Guyot

About Laure

1949

1952

Laure Reichek née *Guyot*

1954

1958

Laure Reichek née *Guyot*

1959

1964

Laure Reichek née Guyot

1976

1994

Laure Reichek née *Guyot*

1994

2008

Laure Reichek née Guyot

2011

2017

Laure Reichek née Guyot

2018

Old Age Reflections

Old and stuck indoors, being quite sound of mind and able of body, gives you time to reflect on your life. What was it for? Do you think the good of it overrode the bad? What are you proud of? Did you accomplish anything you wanted to do? From whom or what did you learn the most? How do you explain your relatively good health and longevity?

My next birthday will be my 90th. I consider that my privileged upbringing in France by my knowledgeable, educated grandparents—in an area of clean air, clean water, fresh local food with close proximity to open spaces, rivers, swamps, forests, shared history, stories, folklore—was the most important factor in my incredible good health. Yet, that area was considered backward by city standards, and the very name of the inhabitants, BERRICHONS, was often used as a synonym for idiot or stupid.

My grandfather chose to practice medicine in this area because it had a great incidence of tuberculosis. This was way before antibiotics had been invented, and he was determined to cure as many infected persons as he could.

When my grandfather declared himself a socialist while in medical school in 1906, his father, a fashionable

Laure Reichek née Guyot

doctor in a large town, disavowed him. My grandfather also made the unforgiveable mistake of falling in love with a woman of the lowest possible caste.

And there was space, lots of space. Everyone had a garden, even the villagers. Dwellings lined the main road on each side, and behind each house was a long empty space where the inhabitants could grow food, keep rabbits and chickens, spaces of coolness in the summer where family and neighbors could gather.

There was a festival every month of the year dedicated and run by a guild of different workers: woodworkers, metalworkers, clockmakers, winemakers, musicians (both traditional and classical). The town had its own municipal band that performed at national and local holidays.

There was a weekly market where foreign goods, as well as local products, were sold on the main square. Though there was no running water or sewer system in the village, many people had wells and hand pumps. For the families of those who did not, the main square had a public pump, where children would line up during their lunch breaks to fill tall, narrow buckets.

Each child was expected to protect and perpetuate the good reputation of his/her family. Reputations were based on one's ability to perform well one's craft or profession. Those who displayed wealth they had not earned were looked down upon. Inherited wealth

Laure Reichek née Guyot

or newly acquired riches were frowned upon. Children owed respect to their parents, all elderly persons and teachers. The best artisans were models to follow, and farmers were judged by how well the farm was kept, not by the size of their farms or flocks.

To be visibly overweight was a sign of sickness or ignorance. There were very few obese persons then, since everyone had to work and people walked from house to field or market; or to church at the end of the town center, about one mile uphill, or to the cemetery even further; or to the lake to wash laundry, more than a mile and pushing a wheelbarrow full of laundry.

Each family had a favorite butcher or baker; there were only two or three of each. Children often did the shopping at their lunch break or after school for meat or bread, since bread was baked twice a day to ensure freshness. Preservatives of any kind were unknown then and would not have been accepted. There were two charcuteries, since processed meats were a separate category from freshly killed animals, which required different training. Charcuteries also made and sold pickles, pâtes of all kinds, hams, sausages; in the fall, there were the meat and products derived from wild animals, such as pheasant, grouse, wild hare, and boar. Ice was delivered in huge blocks to butcher shops and charcuteries and kept in walk-in cold-rooms. No one in town had a refrigerator.

Laure Reichek née Guyot

My grandfather hunted mostly alone with our dog Bobby, a cocker spaniel who lived in the house; Bobby was succeeded by Kimmy. My grandmother made pâtes from the pheasant, grouse, and other wild birds my grandfather brought home. Once a year, he hunted big game with a club of other professionals. They would drive to one of the large forests below the Loire River and spend more than a full day pursuing big game on horseback with a pack of hounds kept separately on our premises, tended and trained at the club's cost. I was forbidden to play with the hounds, but I did anyway, since I could not resist their silky long ears.

On the main square was the emporium where one could buy all notions, as well as pots and pans, baby buggies, prefabricated mattresses and modern furniture. Also in town were the clogmakers, clockmakers, dressmakers, hatmakers, tailors, masons, plasterers, winemakers, woodcutters, farriers, one professional photographer (for weddings), one fabric store, two furniture and cabinetmakers, carpenters, house painters, roofers, and two coopers.

Farmers preferred to have the saddlemaker make their mattresses—mattresses were supposed to last the whole life of the newlyweds and often their offspring. Children would have never thought of using a bed as a trampoline—it would have been the utmost disrespect to the mattress maker and would have endangered the lifespan of the mattress.

Laure Reichek née Guyot

Children obeyed their elders and never argued or talked back when told to do something. It was understood, a priori, that adults knew best, that they had your best interests at heart and you disobeyed at your own peril. You did what you were told, even if it was disagreeable, like swallowing a tablespoon of cod liver oil every morning in the wintertime. Those children—mostly boys—who were unruly were pointed out as "bad children."

An adult male who drank "too much" was considered unworthy of one's company or trade. A man who mistreated his horse was not worth talking to. A man who kept a dirty shop or farm was to be avoided. A woman whose house and children were unkempt was an example not to be followed. One's appearance mattered no matter how poor you were. Water was free, and everyone was to be known to be clean, even when covered with dirt from one's labor.

And then it was 1939.

Men paraded in uniform, singing:

> Y'a Hitler sur la ligne Maginot
> Nos poilus qui l'attendent tout là haut
> Et vrainment si ça lui presse
> Ils lui botterons les fesses
> Y'a Hilter sur la ligne Maginot.

> Hitler's at the Maginot line
> Our men are there waiting for him

And if he's in a hurry to pass
We're going to kick his ass
There's Hitler at the Maginot line.

And men disappeared.

And refugees appeared.

Soldiers in rags were fleeing south.

And I knew, as everyone knew, that our lives would never be the same again and that the change was unpredictable.

The town was bombed.

Mademoiselle Charluteau was killed.

Our doors and windows were blown away.

The larger town where I was in boarding school was bombed, too. I was moved to another school, where we knitted khaki wool mittens and hats for our prisoners-of-war in camps in Germany and for the men sent there in forced labor camps to replace German workers, now soldiers fighting on two fronts.

German armed convoys passed through. More refugees.

Grandpa's car was outfitted with a charcoal burner, since there was no more gasoline.

I was moved again for my safety.

Laure Reichek née Guyot

There were people you no longer spoke to. You were not to talk about certain subjects no matter who asked you questions about the war and what you knew about it.

And then….

Grandpa was killed two months after the Allies landed in Normandy.

And then….

I came back from boarding school to my grandmother's house and stayed there until 1946 when my father came back from war in Indo-China; he placed me in another boarding school outside of Paris, where I stayed until I obtained my BA. My father, who had never been a father, was suddenly forced to worry about me and my sister, now teenagers, and to find a way to organize a life for himself. My sister was sent to prewar friends in Holland as an au pair. I went to London for six months to friends-of-friends, who guaranteed employment and housing and, thus, ration tickets for food.

And then….

I was back in France, attending a drama academy in Paris. It is there I met my future husband, an American ex-soldier studying in Europe on the GI Bill.

And then….

And then….

I came to the US in 1951 when my husband's GI Bill ended, thus ending his four-year study.

And then....

Now, here I am, retracing the steps, filling the gaps, correcting the times and places of events. Not that it matters.

I am the collection of these stories and the millions of details in between, the stories of all the persons I met and those I did not who influenced the way I think and feel; the paintings I saw, the music I heard, the books I read; the landscapes I saw, heard, and smelled, the animals I touched, and places I was privileged to see.

Is that the reason why I have no time to be sick? I have no doctors, I have never been to a hairdresser (I cut my own hair), never been to a nail salon or gym. I thank the sun for coming out every morning, even when I do not see it. I know that it is still there, since I see the consequences of its presence all around me, as I know that all the events of my passage on this earth are the building blocks of the person and personality that I am today.

On the whole, I estimate: Lucky me.

I have been privileged to have been born in a socially advanced country where a modicum of health care and education was available to all born at that time. A country where the revolution was celebrated, and the

Laure Reichek née Guyot

ideas of liberty, equality and fraternity were fostered and encouraged. A place where, yes, bigotry and supremacist views existed, but with active opposition from workers and intellectuals with visions of a more egalitarian society.

Lucky me to have been a teenager in Paris right after WWII and to have been directly exposed to the great men in the arts who were pre-war friends of my father or intellectual soulmates.

Lucky me to have been there in the midst of this creative explosion of ideas repressed during the occupation. Endless discussions in cafés where the only brew was some ersatz of roasted wheat grains and chicory, since foreign trade had not been restored yet. This pseudo-coffee was horrible, but we drank it while smoking homegrown tobacco. We loved the meetings, the gallery openings, the hearts pumping fast and the minds breaking the speed of sound and cultural norms.

Lucky me.

I am grateful to have had the opportunity to see, feel, smell, taste, and hear so much; awed by the variety of people and other species I have encountered.

I am still perplexed by the decisions human beings make in their relations to the planet and the many species of plants and animals that live on it. I still try to understand how we came to the near destruction of our habitat, the intense cruelty that we, as humans,

Laure Reichek née Guyot

are capable of. I have been witness to incredible crimes against humanity and the planet. I have also had the incredible good luck to have been close to great thinkers and artists, creators of magnificent, enriching ideas and works of art.

I am still curious, participating in the fight of good against evil in my small, reduced capacities. I still engage body and mind every day in what I consider "the good" and the "beautiful", meaning social movements for the benefit of the disadvantaged majorities and the tending and protecting of Nature.

I came to this continent to be with a man I would have followed to Siberia or Patagonia. The country hit me in the solar plexus like a heavyweight boxing champion. I was stunned by the unexpected evidence everywhere of obvious, overt racism, open practice of injustice resulting in the incredible gap between rich and poor, privileged and neglected. Chicago, my first home in this country, was difficult to live in with two babies in an illegal basement "apartment" with no windows but many cockroaches, cloth diapers I boiled on the stove and spread to dry over our heads on a line from one end of the room to the other. But I did not care—I was with the man I loved.

Lucky me.

We came to California and I fell in love with the state, especially the North Bay, its hills and coastline.

Laure Reichek née Guyot

I met "good people", thinking and feeling people from a variety of origins, and was actively involved in the creation of a senior center, a homeless shelter, and an organization to help immigrant working women. I have worked as a volunteer in public schools as a mentor and volunteered in a restaurant as a prep cook. I have tended the land on which I live and formed relationships with animals.

Lucky me.

The bad memories are quickly pushed back by the good ones of the beauty I have seen on the planet and the kindness of the people who have educated me, stimulated my mind and fed my body, thankful to nature that accepted my presence for so long and rewarded me with longevity.

Oh! Lucky me!

My two children, now bald and middle-aged, have become good men; they taught me patience, tolerance, and acceptance of their own histories.

Oh, lucky me!

For that I am thankful.

Oh! Lucky me!

I have fallen in love many times but really loved deeply only once, and it was my luck to have been able to live with that man more than 60 years. I miss him every day. I have been loved deeply by my grandparents

Laure Reichek née Guyot

and received a great deal of affection from many people unrelated to me. Many others have shown appreciation for my involvements in civic and political matters; I was glad to have the chance to serve. I hope that I have not caused any harm or pain to anyone; I have tried not to, even when I disagreed and forcefully expressed it. I think that Nature has given me more than I could ever give to Her.

How lucky can a human be with all the design faults of an unfinished, badly managed experiment?

How lucky to have been exposed to better proposals for the management of human affairs and ideas of better relations with the rest of the planet.

How lucky!

P.S. I wish all living beings as good a life as I have had. The good and the bad, evil and kindness, selfishness and altruism, ugliness and beauty. One learns from the encounter of both.

Laure Reichek née Guyot

Acknowledgements

Petaluma, CA, USA, 2018

These stories were originally written and edited by Laure Reichek long hand-cursive, using a ball point pen.

Mr Sotton

I do not know whether I could find the way to Mr Sotton's house in the forest - I had never gone there alone - I was a child then. But I would like to think that if someone pointed me in the right direction I would find my way - The way ~~people~~ birds do. First the small dirt road, on the right it was, in the middle of the forest. Then perhaps a mile further in, with ditches on both sides, the uneven ground you suddenly come to a clearing - And there it is on the right, in the center of the clearing - A square house made of stone with two steps in front Inside, just one room. A chimney, a table and benches, a bed, an armoire - Just one room, almost

In 2016, Barbara Crum of Watsonville, California, spent 4 visits of 3–4 days each, over the course of the year, in Petaluma with Laure. During that time, Barbara read the stories on the paper on which they were originally written and edited by Laure.

After reading each story, Barbara did a preliminary transcription using a laptop computer and printed the results to hardcopy. With the original hand-written

Laure Reichek née *Guyot*

story and a hardcopy of the initial transcription in front of them laid out on the main table in the main room of Laure's home, Barbara and Laure went over the stories, sentence by sentence and word by word, resulting in another hardcopy of the story to continue to compare and conform to the original handwritten work. This was repeated 3–4 times for each story.

During this year-long collaboration, Laure would occasionally read aloud to Barbara an entire story or a few paragraphs at a time to confirm the flow and rhythm of the story.

In 2017, Elizabeth Baker went through the editorial and computer work Barbara had done the previous year. Over a period of several weeks, Elizabeth focused on typos and grammatical errors, further refining the transcribed work.

In 2018 Joshua Reichek created a website from the computer versions of the stories, including a few readily available relevant pictures. Through 2019, he continued to work on and refine the website, verifying research, and locating additional relevant images. In the late fall of 2019, Joshua and Elizabeth began the process of converting the website to hardcopy book form as a self-publishing effort. The work was completed in September of 2020. Final proof reading and editorial was done by Barbara Crum and Elizabeth Baker. The book was first emailed to the printers on May 16, 2020, the 69th wedding anniversary of Laure and Jesse.

Laure Reichek née *Guyot*

Autrefois

Une beurriere Berrichonne

churning butter

Laure Reichek née Guyot

Talbot, éditeur

510 — Argent (Cher) - Une Argentaise de 97 ans

97-year-old woman from Argent

Laure Reichek née Guyot

Argent

Laure Reichek née Guyot

horse exchange

fairground, Bosnay

Laure Reichek née *Guyot*

calf market

Market Hall

Laure Reichek née Guyot

day of the market

market, St-Amand-Montrond

Laure Reichek née Guyot

main street, Argenton

main street, Châteauroux

Laure Reichek née Guyot

main street, Vierzon

main street, Bourges

Laure Reichek née Guyot

avenue to the rail station, Châteauroux

pâtisserie, Châteauroux

Laure Reichek née Guyot

main street, Levroux

travellers' hotel, Orsennes

Laure Reichek née *Guyot*

main street and Aux Printemps, Le Blanc

Magasins Modernes, a department store

Manufacture Nationale des Tabaces

brewery, Châteauroux

Laure Reichek née Guyot

C. Talichet sawmill, Châteauroux

M. Bourin sawmill, Poulnay

Laure Reichek née Guyot

horseshoeing at the forge

washerwoman

Laure Reichek née *Guyot*

potters, La Borne

harvesting the hay

Laure Reichek née *Guyot*

bringing in the hay

field labor

Laure Reichek née Guyot

plowing

a plowman and his horses

Laure Reichek née Guyot

Berry   Joueur de Vielle.

minstrel with hurdy-gurdy

**All historical pictures of postcards
(except the postcard of Chateaumaillant on page 3)
are reprinted from "Le Berry D'Autrefois ",
by Jean-Louis Boncoeur
Editions Horvath 21 November 1980**

Laure Reichek née *Guyot*

Eglise de Nohant
watercolor by Laure, age 9
December 1940